DONATION

BEOWULF

Beowulf

Translated by SEAMUS HEANEY

faber and faber

First published in 1999
by Faber and Faber Limited
3 Queen Square London WC1N 3AU

Photoset by Parker Typesetting Service, Leicester
Printed in England by Clays Ltd, St Ives plc

Seamus Heaney is hereby identified as translator
of this work in accordance with Section 77
of the Copyright, Designs and Patents Act 1988

A CIP record for this book
is available from the British Library

ISBN 0–571–20113–X (cased)
ISBN 0–571–20342–6 (limited edition)

10 9 8 7 6 5 4

In memory of Ted Hughes

CONTENTS

And now this is 'an inheritance' –
Upright, rudimentary, unshiftably planked
In the long ago, yet willable forward

Again and again and again.

1 BEOWULF: THE POEM

The poem called *Beowulf* was composed some time between
the middle of the seventh and the end of the tenth century of
the first millennium, in the language that is today called
Anglo-Saxon or Old English. It is a heroic narrative, more
than three thousand lines long, concerning the deeds of a
Scandinavian prince, also called Beowulf, and it stands as one
of the foundation works of poetry in English. The fact that the
English language has changed so much in the last thousand
years means, however, that the poem is now generally read in
translation and mostly in English courses at schools and uni-
versities. This has contributed to the impression that it was
written (as Osip Mandelstam said of *The Divine Comedy*) 'on
official paper', which is unfortunate, since what we are dealing
with is a work of the greatest imaginative vitality, a master-
piece where the structuring of the tale is as elaborate as the
beautiful contrivances of its language. Its narrative elements
may belong to a previous age but as a work of art it lives in its
own continuous present, equal to our knowledge of reality in
the present time.

The poem was written in England but the events it describes
are set in Scandinavia, in a 'once upon a time' that is partly
historical. Its hero, Beowulf, is the biggest presence among the
warriors in the land of the Geats, a territory situated in what is
now southern Sweden, and early in the poem Beowulf crosses
the sea to the land of the Danes in order to rid their country of

a man-eating monster called Grendel. From this expedition (which involves him in a second contest with Grendel's mother) he returns in triumph and eventually rules for fifty years as king of his homeland. Then a dragon begins to terrorize the countryside and Beowulf must confront it. In a final climactic encounter, he does manage to slay the dragon, but he also meets his own death and enters the legends of his people as a warrior of high renown.

We know about the poem more or less by chance, because it exists in one manuscript only. This unique copy (now in the British Library) barely survived a fire in the eighteenth century and was then transcribed and titled, retranscribed and edited, translated and adapted, interpreted and taught, until it has become an acknowledged classic. For decades it has been a set book on English syllabuses at university level all over the world. The fact that many English departments require it to be studied in the original continues to generate resistance, most notably at Oxford University, where the pros and cons of the inclusion of part of it as a compulsory element in the English course have been debated regularly in recent years.

For generations of undergraduates, academic study of the poem was often just a matter of construing the meaning, getting a grip on the grammar and vocabulary of Anglo-Saxon, and being able to recognize, translate and comment upon random extracts that were presented in the examinations. For generations of scholars too the interest had been textual and philological; then there developed a body of research into analogues and sources, a quest for stories and episodes in the folklore and legends of the Nordic peoples that would parallel or foreshadow episodes in *Beowulf*. Scholars were also preoccupied with fixing the exact time and place of the poem's composition, paying minute attention to linguistic, stylistic and scribal details. More generally, they tried to establish the history and genealogy of the dynasties of Swedes, Geats and Danes to which the poet makes constant allusion; and they devoted themselves to a consideration of the world-view behind the poem, asking to what extent (if at all) the newly established Christian religion, which was fundamental to the poet's intellectual formation, displaced him from his imaginative at-homeness in the world of his poem – a pagan Germanic society governed by a heroic code of honour, one where the attainment of a name for warrior-prowess among the living overwhelms any concern about the soul's destiny in the afterlife.

However, when it comes to considering *Beowulf* as a work of literature, one publication stands out. In 1936, the Oxford scholar and teacher J. R. R. Tolkien published an epoch-making paper entitled '*Beowulf:* The Monsters and the Critics', which took for granted the poem's integrity and distinction as a work of art and proceeded to show in what this integrity and distinction inhered. Tolkien assumed that the poet had felt his way through the inherited material – the fabulous elements and the traditional accounts of an heroic past – and by a combination of creative intuition and conscious structuring had arrived at a unity of effect and a balanced order. He assumed, in other words, that the *Beowulf* poet was an imaginative writer rather than some kind of back-formation derived from nineteenth-century folklore and philology. Tolkien's brilliant literary treatment changed the way the poem was valued and initiated a new era – and new terms – of appreciation.

It is impossible to attain a full understanding and estimate of *Beowulf* without recourse to this immense body of commentary and elucidation. Nevertheless, readers coming to the poem for the first time are likely to experience something other than mere discomfiture when faced with the strangeness of the names and the immediate lack of known reference points. An English-speaker new to *The Iliad* or *The Odyssey* or *The Aeneid* will probably at least have heard of Troy and Helen, or of Penelope and the Cyclops, or of Dido and the Golden Bough. These epics may be in Greek and Latin, yet the classical heritage has entered the cultural memory enshrined in English so thoroughly that their worlds are more familiar than that of the first native epic, even though it was composed centuries after them. Achilles rings a bell, but not *Scyld Scēfing*. Ithaca leads the mind in a certain direction, but not *Heorot*. The Sibyl of Cumae will stir certain associations, but not bad Queen Modthryth. First-time readers of *Beowulf* very quickly rediscover the meaning of the term 'the Dark Ages', and it is in the hope of dispelling some of the puzzlement they are bound to feel that I have added the marginal glosses that appear in the following pages.

Still, in spite of the sensation of being caught between a 'shield-wall' of opaque references and a 'word-hoard' that is old and strange, such readers are also bound to feel a certain 'shock of the new'. This is because the poem possesses a mythic potency. Like Shield Sheafson (as *Scyld Scēfing* is known in this translation), it arrives from somewhere beyond the known bourne of our experience, and having fulfilled its purpose (again like Shield) it passes once more into the beyond. In the intervening time, the poet conjures up a work as remote as Shield's funeral boat borne towards the horizon, as commanding as the horn-pronged gables of King Hrothgar's hall, as solid and dazzling as Beowulf's funeral pyre that is set ablaze at the end. These opening and closing scenes retain a haunting presence in the mind; they are set pieces but they have the life-marking power of certain dreams. They are like the pillars of the gate of horn, through which the wise dreams of true art can still be said to pass.

What happens in between is what W. B. Yeats would have called a phantasmagoria. Three agons – three struggles in which the preternatural force-for-evil of the hero's enemies comes springing at him in demonic shapes; three encounters with what the critical literature and the textbook glossaries call 'the monsters' – in three archetypal sites of fear: the barricaded night-house, the infested underwater current and the reptile-haunted rocks of a wilderness. If we think of the poem in this way, its place in world art becomes clearer and more secure. We can conceive of it re-presented and transformed in performance in a *bunraku* theatre in Japan, where the puppetry and the poetry are mutually supportive, a mixture of technicolor spectacle and ritual chant. Or we can equally envisage it as an animated cartoon (and there has been at least one shot at this already), full of mutating graphics and minatory stereophonics. We can avoid, at any rate, the slightly cardboard effect that the word 'monster' tends to introduce, and give the poem a fresh chance to sweep 'in off the moors, down through the mist-bands' of Anglo-Saxon England, forward into the global village of the third millennium.

Nevertheless, the dream element and overall power to haunt come at a certain readerly price. The poem abounds in passages that will leave an unprepared audience bewildered. Just when the narrative seems ready to take another step ahead, it sidesteps. For a moment it is as if we have been channel-surfed into another poem, and at two points in this translation I indicate that we are in fact participating in a poem-within-our-poem not only by the use of italics, but by a slight quickening of pace and shortening of metrical rein. The passages comprise lines 883–914 and 1070–158, and on each occasion a minstrel has begun to chant a poem as part of the celebration of Beowulf's achievements. In the former case, the minstrel expresses his praise by telling the story of Sigemund's victory over a dragon, which both parallels Beowulf's triumph over Grendel and prefigures his fatal encounter with the *wyrm* in his old age. In the latter – the most famous of what were once called the 'digressions' in the poem, the one dealing with a fight between Danes and Frisians at the stronghold of Finn, the Frisian king – the song the minstrel sings has a less obvious bearing on the immediate situation of the hero, but its import is nevertheless central to both the historical and imaginative worlds of the poem.

The 'Finnsburg episode' immerses us in a society that is at once honour-bound and blood-stained, presided over by the laws of the blood-feud, where the kin of a person slain are bound to exact a price for the death, either by slaying the killer or by receiving satisfaction in the form of *wergild* (the 'man-price'), a legally fixed compensation. The claustrophobic and doom-laden atmosphere of this interlude gives the reader an intense intimation of what *wyrd*, or fate, meant not only to the characters in the Finn story but to those participating in the main action of *Beowulf* itself. All conceive of themselves as hooped within the great wheel of necessity, in thrall to a code of loyalty and bravery, bound to seek glory in the eye of the warrior world. The little nations are grouped around their lord; the greater nations spoil for war and menace the little ones; a lord dies, defencelessness ensues; the enemy strikes; vengeance for the dead becomes an ethic for the living, bloodshed begets further bloodshed; the wheel turns, the generations tread and tread and tread – which is what I meant above when I said that the import of the Finnsburg passage is central to the historical and imaginative worlds of the poem as a whole

One way of reading *Beowulf* is to think of it as three agons in the hero's life, but another way would be to regard it as a poem that contemplates the destinies of three peoples by tracing their interweaving histories in the story of the central character. First we meet the Danes – variously known as the Shieldings (after Shield Sheafson, the founder of their line), the Ingwins, the Spear-Danes, the Bright-Danes, the West-Danes, and so on – a people in the full summer of their power, symbolized by the high hall built by King Hrothgar, one 'meant to be a wonder of the world'. The threat to this superb people comes from within their own borders, from marshes beyond the pale, from the bottom of the haunted mere where 'Cain's clan', in the shape of Grendel and his troll-dam, trawl and scavenge and bide their time. But it also comes from without, from the Heathobards, for example, whom the Danes have defeated in battle and from whom they can therefore expect retaliatory war (see lines 2020–69).

Beowulf actually predicts this turn of events when he goes back to his own country after saving the Danes (for the time being, at any rate) by staving off the two 'reavers from hell'. In the hall of his 'ring-giver', Hygelac, lord of the Geats, the hero discourses about his adventures in a securely fortified cliff-top enclosure. But this security is only temporary, for it is the destiny of the Geat people to be left lordless in the end. Hygelac's alliances eventually involve him in deadly war with the Swedish king, Ongentheow, and even though he does not personally deliver the fatal stroke (two of his thanes are responsible for this – see lines 2484–9 and then the lengthier reprise of this incident at lines 2922–3003), he is known in the poem as 'Ongentheow's killer'. Hence it comes to pass that after the death of Beowulf, who eventually succeeds Hygelac, the Geats experience a great foreboding and the poem closes in a mood of sombre expectation. A world is passing away, the Swedes and others are massing on the borders to attack and there is no lord or hero to rally the defence.

The Swedes, therefore, are the third nation whose history and destiny are woven into the narrative, and even though no part of the main action is set in their territory, they and their kings constantly stalk the horizon of dread within which the main protagonists pursue their conflicts and allegiances. The Swedish dimension gradually becomes an important element in the poem's emotional and imaginative geography, a geography that entails, it should be said, no very clear map-sense of the world, more an apprehension of menaced borders, of danger gathering beyond the mere and the marshes, of *mearc-sta-pas* 'prowling the moors, huge marauders / from some other world'.

Within these phantasmal boundaries, each lord's hall is an actual and a symbolic refuge. Here are heat and light, rank and ceremony, human solidarity and culture; the *duguþ* share the mead-benches with the *geogoþ*, the veterans with their tales of warrior-kings and hero-saviours from the past rub shoulders with young braves – *þegnas, eorlas*, thanes, retainers – keen to win such renown in the future. The prospect of gaining a glorious name in the *wæl-ræs* (the rush of battle-slaughter), the pride of defending one's lord and bearing heroic witness to the integrity of the bond between him and his hall-companions – a bond sealed in the *glēo* and *gidd* of peace-time feasting and ring-giving – this is what gave drive and sanction to the Germanic warrior-culture enshrined in *Beowulf*.

Heorot and Hygelac's hall are the hubs of this value system upon which the poem's action turns. But there is another, outer rim of value, a circumference of understanding within which the heroic world is occasionally viewed as from a distance and recognized for what it is, an earlier state of consciousness and culture, one that has not been altogether shed but that has now been comprehended as part of another pattern. And this circumference and pattern arise, of course, from the poet's Christianity and from his perspective as an Englishman looking back at places and legends that his ancestors knew before they made their migration from continental Europe to their new home on the island of the Britons. As a consequence of his doctrinal certitude, which is as composed as it is ardent, the poet can view the story-time of his poem with a certain historical detachment and even censure the ways of those who lived *in illo tempore*:

> Sometimes at pagan shrines they vowed
> offerings to idols, swore oaths
> that the killer of souls might come to their aid
> and save the people. That was their way,
> their heathenish hope; deep in their hearts
> they remembered hell.

[175–80]

At the same time, as a result of his inherited vernacular culture and the imaginative sympathy that distinguishes him as an artist, the poet can lend the full weight of his rhetorical power to Beowulf as he utters the first principles of the northern warrior's honour-code:

> It is always better
> to avenge dear ones than to indulge in mourning.
> For every one of us, living in this world

means waiting for our end. Let whoever can
win glory before death. When a warrior is gone,
that will be his best and only bulwark.   [1384–9]

In an age when 'the instability of the human subject' is con-
stantly argued for if not presumed, there should be no pro-
blem with a poem that is woven from two such different
psychic fabrics. In fact, *Beowulf* perfectly answers the early
modern conception of a work of creative imagination as one
in which conflicting realities find accommodation within a
new order; and this reconciliation occurs, it seems to me, most
poignantly and most profoundly in the poem's third section,
once the dragon enters the picture and the hero in old age
must gather his powers for the final climactic ordeal. From the
moment Beowulf advances under the crags, into the comfort-
less arena bounded by the rock-wall, the reader knows he is
one of those 'marked by fate'. The poetry is imbued with a
strong intuition of *wyrd* hovering close, 'unknowable but cer-
tain', and yet, because it is imagined within a consciousness
that has learned to expect that the soul will find an ultimate
home 'among the steadfast ones', this primal human emotion
has been transmuted into something less 'zero at the bone',
more metaphysically tempered.

A similar transposition from a plane of regard that is, as it
were, helmeted and hall-bound to one that sees things in a
slightly more heavenly light is discernible in the different ways
the poet imagines gold. Gold is a constant element, gleaming
solidly in underground vaults, on the breasts of queens or the
arms and regalia of warriors on the mead-benches. It is loaded
into boats as spoil, handed out in bent bars as hall-gifts, buried
in the earth as treasure, persisting underground as an affirma-
tion of a people's glorious past and an elegy for it. It pervades
the ethos of the poem and adds lustre to its diction. And yet
the bullion with which Waels's son Sigemund weighs down
the hold after an earlier dragon-slaying triumph (in the old
days, long before Beowulf's time) is a more trustworthy sub-

stance than that which is secured behind the walls of Beowulf's barrow. By the end of the poem, gold has suffered a radiation from the Christian vision. It is not that it yet equals riches in the medieval sense of worldly corruption, just that its status as the ore of all value has been put in doubt. It is *læne*, transitory, passing from hand to hand, and its changed status is registered as a symptom of the changed world. Once the dragon is disturbed, the melancholy and sense of displacement that pervade the last movement of the poem enter the hoard as a disabling and ominous light. And the dragon himself, as a genius of the older order, is bathed in this light, so that even as he begins to stir, the reader has a premonition that the days of his empery are numbered.

Nevertheless, the dragon has a wonderful inevitability about him and a unique glamour. It is not that the other monsters are lacking in presence and aura; it is more that they remain, for all their power to terrorize, creatures of the physical world. Grendel comes alive in the reader's imagination as a kind of dog-breath in the dark, a fear of collision with some hard-boned and immensely strong android frame, a mixture of Caliban and hoplite. And while his mother too has a definite brute-bearing about her, a creature of slouch and lunge on land if seal-swift in the water, she nevertheless retains a certain non-strangeness. As antagonists of a hero being tested, Grendel and his mother possess an appropriate head-on strength. The poet may need them as figures who do the devil's work, but the poem needs them more as figures who call up and show off Beowulf's physical strength and his superb gifts as a warrior. They are the right enemies for a young glory-hunter, instigators of the formal boast, worthy trophies to be carried back from the grim testing-ground – Grendel's hand is ripped off and nailed up, his head severed and paraded in Heorot. It is all consonant with the surge of youth and the compulsion to win fame 'as wide as the wind's home, / as the sea around cliffs', utterly a manifestation of the Germanic heroic code.

Enter then, fifty years later, the dragon – from his dry-stone vault, from a nest where he is heaped in coils around the body-heated gold. Once he is wakened, there is something glorious in the way he manifests himself, a Fourth of July effulgence fireworking its path across the night sky; and yet, because of the centuries he has spent dormant in the tumulus, there is a foundedness as well as a lambency about him. He is at once a stratum of the earth and a streamer in the air, no painted dragon but a figure of real oneiric power, one that can easily survive the prejudice that arises at the very mention of the word 'dragon'. Whether in medieval art or modern Disney cartoons, the dragon can strike us as far less horrific than he is meant to be, but in the final movement of *Beowulf* he lodges himself in the imagination as *wyrd* rather than *wyrm*, more a destiny than a set of reptilian vertebrae.

Grendel and his mother enter Beowulf's life from the outside, accidentally, challenges which in other circumstances he might not have taken up, enemies from whom he might have been distracted or deflected. The dragon, on the other hand, is a given of his home ground, abiding in his under-earth as in his understanding, waiting for the meeting, the watcher at the ford, the questioner who sits so sly, the 'lion-limb', as Gerard Manley Hopkins might have called him, against whom Beowulf's body and soul must measure themselves. Dragon equals shadow-line, the psalmist's valley of the shadow of death, the embodiment of a knowledge deeply ingrained in the species – the knowledge, that is, of the price to be paid for physical and spiritual survival.

It has often been observed that all the scriptural references in *Beowulf* are to the Old Testament. The poet is more in sympathy with the tragic, waiting, unredeemed phase of things than with any transcendental promise. Beowulf's mood as he gets ready to fight the dragon – who could be read as a projection of Beowulf's own chthonic wisdom refined in the crucible of experience – recalls the mood of other tragic heroes: Oedipus at Colonus, Lear at his 'ripeness is all' extremity, Hamlet in the last illuminations of his 'prophetic soul':

> no easy bargain
> would be made in that place by any man.
> The veteran king sat down on the cliff-top.
> He wished good luck to the Geats who had shared
> his hearth and his gold. He was sad at heart,
> unsettled yet ready, sensing his death.
> His fate hovered near, unknowable but certain.

[2415–21]

Here the poet attains a level of insight that approaches the visionary. The subjective and the inevitable are in perfect balance, what is solidly established is bathed in an element that is completely sixth-sensed, and indeed the whole, slow-motion, constantly self-deferring approach to the hero's death and funeral continues to be like this. Beowulf's soul may not yet have fled 'to its destined place among the steadfast ones', but there is already a beyond-the-grave aspect to him, a revenant quality about his resoluteness. This is not just metrical narrative full of anthropological interest and typical heroic-age motifs; it is poetry of a high order, in which passages of great lyric intensity – such as the 'Lay of the Last Survivor' (lines 2247–66) and, even more remarkably, the so-called 'Father's Lament' (2444–62) – rise like emanations from some fissure in the bedrock of the human capacity to endure:

> It was like the misery endured by an old man
> who has lived to see his son's body
> swing on the gallows. He begins to keen
> and weep for his boy, watching the raven
> gloat where he hangs; he can be of no help.
> The wisdom of age is worthless to him.
> Morning after morning, he wakes to remember
> that his child is gone; he has no interest
> in living on until another heir
> is born in the hall . . .
> Alone with his longing, he lies down on his bed
> and sings a lament; everything seems too large,
> the steadings and the fields.

[2444–53, 2460–2]

Such passages mark an ultimate stage in poetic attainment; they are the imaginative equivalent of Beowulf's spiritual state at the end, when he tells his men that 'doom of battle will bear [their] lord away', in the same way that the sea-journeys so vividly described in lines 210–28 and lines 1903–24 are the equivalent of his exultant prime.

At these moments of lyric intensity, the keel of the poetry is deeply set in the element of sensation while the mind's lookout sways metrically and far-sightedly in the element of pure comprehension – which is to say that the elevation of *Beowulf* is always, paradoxically, buoyantly down-to-earth. And nowhere is this more obviously and memorably the case than in the account of the hero's funeral with which the poem ends. Here the inexorable and the elegiac combine in a description of the funeral pyre being got ready, the body being burnt and the barrow being constructed – a scene at once immemorial and oddly contemporary. The Geat woman who cries out in dread as the flames consume the body of her dead lord could come straight from a late-twentieth-century news report, from Rwanda or Kosovo; her keen is a nightmare glimpse into the minds of people who have survived traumatic, even monstrous events and who are now being exposed to a comfortless future. We immediately recognize her predicament and the pitch of her grief and find ourselves the better for having them expressed with such adequacy, dignity and unforgiving truth:

On a height they kindled the hugest of all
funeral fires; fumes of woodsmoke
billowed darkly up, the blaze roared
and drowned out their weeping, wind died down
and flames wrought havoc in the hot bone-house,
burning it to the core. They were disconsolate
and wailed aloud for their lord's decease.
A Geat woman too sang out in grief;
with hair bound up, she unburdened herself
of her worst fears, a wild litany

of nightmare and lament: her nation invaded,
enemies on the rampage, bodies in piles,
slavery and abasement. Heaven swallowed the smoke.

2 ABOUT THIS TRANSLATION

When I was an undergraduate at Queen's University, Belfast, I studied *Beowulf* and other Anglo-Saxon poems and developed not only a feel for the language, but a fondness for the melancholy and fortitude that characterized the poetry. Consequently, when an invitation to translate the poem arrived from the editors of *The Norton Anthology of English Literature*, I was tempted to try my hand. While I had no great expertise in Old English, I had a strong desire to get back to the first stratum of the language and to 'assay the hoard' (line 2509). This was during the middle years of the 1980s, when I had begun a regular teaching job in Harvard and was opening my ear to the unmoored speech of some contemporary American poetry. Saying yes to the *Beowulf* commission would be (I argued with myself) a kind of aural antidote, a way of ensuring that my linguistic anchor would stay lodged on the Anglo-Saxon sea-floor. So I undertook to do it.

Very soon, however, I hesitated. It was labour-intensive work, scriptorium-slow. I proceeded dutifully like a sixth-former at homework. I would set myself twenty lines a day, write out my glossary of hard words in longhand, try to pick a way through the syntax, get the run of the meaning established in my head and then hope that the lines could be turned into metrical shape and raised to the power of verse. Often, however, the whole attempt to turn it into modern English seemed to me like trying to bring down a megalith with a toy hammer. What had been so attractive in the first place, the hand-built, rock-sure feel of the thing, began to defeat me. I turned to other work, the commissioning editors did not pursue me, and the project went into abeyance.

Even so, I had an instinct that it should not be let go. An understanding I had worked out for myself concerning my own linguistic and literary origins made me reluctant to abandon the task. I had noticed, for example, that without any conscious intent on my part certain lines in the first poem in my first book conformed to the requirements of Anglo-Saxon metrics. These lines were made up of two balancing halves, each half containing two stressed syllables – 'The spade sinks   into gravelly ground: / My father digging.   I look down . . .' – and in the case of the second line there was alliteration linking 'digging' and 'down' across the caesura. Part of me, in other words, had been writing Anglo-Saxon from the start.

This was not surprising, given that the poet who had first formed my ear was Gerard Manley Hopkins. Hopkins was a chip off the Old English block, and the earliest lines I published when I was a student were as much pastiche Anglo-Saxon as they were pastiche Hopkins: 'Starling thatch-watches and sudden swallow / Straight breaks to mud-nest, home-rest rafter', and so on. I have written about all this elsewhere and about the relation of my Hopkins ventriloquism to the speech patterns of Ulster – especially as these were caricatured by the poet W. R. Rodgers. Ulster people, according to Rodgers, are 'an abrupt people / who like the spiky consonants of speech / and think the soft ones cissy', and get a kick out of 'anything that gives or takes attack / like Micks, Teagues, tinkers' gets, Vatican'.

Joseph Brodsky once said that poets' biographies are present in the sounds they make and I suppose all I am saying is that I consider *Beowulf* to be part of my voice-right. And yet to persuade myself that I was born into its language and that its language was born into me took a while: for somebody who grew up in the political and cultural conditions of Lord Brookeborough's Northern Ireland, it could hardly have been otherwise.

Sprung from an Irish nationalist background and educated at a Northern Irish Catholic school, I had learned the Irish language and lived within a cultural and ideological frame that regarded it as the language that I should by rights have been speaking but I had been robbed of. I have also written, for example, about the thrill I experienced when I stumbled upon the word *lachtar* in my Irish-English dictionary, and found that this word, which my aunt had always used when speaking of a flock of chicks, was in fact an Irish language word, and more than that, an Irish word associated in particular with County Derry. Yet here it was, surviving in my aunt's English speech generations after her forebears and mine had ceased to speak Irish. For a long time, therefore, the little word was – to borrow a simile from Joyce – like a rapier point of consciousness pricking me with an awareness of language-loss and cultural dispossession, and tempting me into binary thinking about language. I tended to conceive of English and Irish as adversarial tongues, as either/or conditions rather than both/and, and this was an attitude that for a long time hampered the development of a more confident and creative way of dealing with the whole vexed question – the question, that is, of the relationship between nationality, language, history and literary tradition in Ireland.

Luckily, I glimpsed the possibility of release from this kind of cultural determination early on, in my first arts year at Queen's University, Belfast, when we were lectured on the history of the English Language by Professor John Braidwood. Braidwood could not help informing us, for example, that the word 'whiskey' is the same word as the Irish and Scots Gaelic word *uisce*, meaning water, and that the River Usk in Britain is therefore to some extent the River Uisce (or Whiskey); and so in my mind the stream was suddenly turned into a kind of linguistic river of rivers issuing from a pristine Celto-British Land of Cockaigne, a riverrun of Finnegans Wakespeak pouring out of the cleft rock of some prepolitical, prelapsarian, ur-philological Big Rock Candy Mountain – and all of this had a wonderfully sweetening effect upon me. The Irish/English duality, the Celtic/Saxon antithesis were momentarily collapsed and in the resulting etymological eddy a gleam of recognition flashed through the synapses and I glimpsed an elsewhere of potential that seemed at the same time to be a somewhere being remembered. The place on the language map where the Usk and the *uisce* and the whiskey coincided was definitely a place where the spirit might find a loophole, an escape route from what John Montague has called 'the partitioned intellect', away into some unpartitioned linguistic country, a region where one's language would not be simply a badge of ethnicity or a matter of cultural preference or an official imposition, but an entry into further language. And I eventually came upon one of these loopholes in *Beowulf* itself.

What happened was that I found in the glossary to C. L. Wrenn's edition of the poem the Old English word meaning 'to suffer', the word *þolian*; and although at first it looked completely strange with its *thorn* symbol instead of the familiar *th*, I gradually realized that it was not strange at all, for it was the word that older and less educated people would have used in the country where I grew up. 'They'll just have to learn to thole,' my aunt would say about some family who had suffered an unforeseen bereavement. And now suddenly here was 'thole' in the official textual world, mediated through the apparatus of a scholarly edition, a little bleeper to remind me that my aunt's language was not just a self-enclosed family possession but an historical heritage, one that involved the journey *þolian* had made north into Scotland and then across into Ulster with the planters, and then across from the planters to the locals who had originally spoken Irish, and then farther across again when the Scots Irish emigrated to the American South in the eighteenth century. When I read in John Crowe Ransom the line, 'Sweet ladies, long may ye bloom, and toughly I hope ye may thole', my heart lifted again, the world widened, something was furthered. The far-flungness of the word, the phenomenological pleasure of finding it variously transformed by Ransom's modernity and *Beowulf*'s venerability made me feel vaguely something for which again I only found the words years later. What I was experiencing as I kept meeting up with *thole* on its multi-cultural odyssey was the feeling that Osip Mandelstam once defined as a 'nostalgia for world culture'. And this was a nostalgia I didn't even know I suffered until I experienced its fulfilment in this little epiphany. It was as if, on the analogy of baptism by desire, I had undergone something like illumination by philology. And even though I did not know it at the time, I had by then reached the point where I was ready to translate *Beowulf*. *Þolian* had opened my right of way.

So, in a sense, the decision to accept Norton's invitation was taken thirty-five years before the invitation was actually issued. But between one's sense of readiness to take on a subject and the actual inscription of the first lines, there is always a problematical hiatus. To put it another way: from the point of view of the writer, words in a poem need what the Polish poet Anna Swir once called 'the equivalent of a biological right to life'. The erotics of composition are essential to the process, some prereflective excitation and orientation, some sense that your own little verse-craft can dock safe and sound at the big quay of the language. And this is as true for translators as it is for poets attempting original work.

It is one thing to find lexical meanings for the words and to have some feel for how the metre might go, but it is quite another thing to find the tuning fork that will give you the note and pitch for the overall music of the work. Without some melody sensed or promised, it is simply impossible for a poet to establish the translator's right of way into and through a text. I was therefore lucky to hear this enabling note almost straight away, a familiar local voice, one that had belonged to relatives of my father, people whom I had once described (punning on their surname) as 'big-voiced scullions'.

I called them 'big-voiced' because when the men of the family spoke, the words they uttered came across with a weighty distinctness, phonetic units as separate and defined as delph platters displayed on a dresser shelf. A simple sentence such as 'We cut the corn today' took on immense dignity when one of the Scullions spoke it. They had a kind of Native American solemnity of utterance, as if they were announcing verdicts rather than making small talk. And when I came to ask myself how I wanted *Beowulf* to sound in my version, I realized I wanted it to be speakable by one of those relatives. I therefore tried to frame the famous opening lines in cadences that would have suited their voices, but that still echoed with the sound and sense of the Anglo-Saxon:

> Hwæt wē Gār-Dena   in gēar-dagum
> þēod-cyninga   þrym gefrūnon,
> hū þā æþelingas   ellen fremedon.

Conventional renderings of *hwæt*, the first word of the poem, tend towards the archaic literary, with 'lo', 'hark', 'behold', 'attend' and – more colloquially – 'listen' being some of the solutions offered previously. But in Hiberno-English Scullion-speak, the particle 'so' came naturally to the rescue, because in that idiom 'so' operates as an expression that obliterates all previous discourse and narrative, and at the same time functions as an exclamation calling for immediate attention. So, 'so' it was:

> So. The Spear-Danes in days gone by
> and the kings who ruled them had courage and greatness.
> We have heard of those princes' heroic campaigns.

I came to the task of translating *Beowulf* with a prejudice in favour of forthright delivery. I remembered the voice of the poem as being attractively direct, even though the diction was ornate and the narrative method at times oblique. What I had always loved was a kind of foursquareness about the utterance, a feeling of living inside a constantly indicative mood, in the presence of an understanding that assumes you share an awareness of the perilous nature of life and are yet capable of seeing it steadily and, when necessary, sternly. There is an undeluded quality about the *Beowulf* poet's sense of the world that gives his lines immense emotional credibility and allows him to make general observations about life that are far too grounded in experience and reticence to be called 'moralizing'. These so-called 'gnomic' parts of the poem have the cadence and force of earned wisdom, and their combination of cogency and verity was again something that I could remember from the speech I heard as a youngster in the Scullion kitchen. When I translate lines 24–5 as 'Behaviour that's admired / is the path to power among people everywhere', I am attending as much to the grain of my original vernacular as to the content of the Anglo-Saxon lines. But then the evidence suggests that this middle ground between oral tradition and the demands of written practice was also the ground occupied by the *Beowulf* poet. The style of the poem is hospitable to the kind of formulaic phrases that are the stock-in-trade of oral bards, and yet it is marked too by the self-consciousness of an artist convinced that 'we must labour to be beautiful'.

In one area, my own labours have been less than thorough-going. I have not followed the strict metrical rules that bound the Anglo-Saxon *scop*. I have been guided by the fundamental pattern of four stresses to the line, but I allow myself several transgressions. For example, I don't always employ alliteration, and sometimes I alliterate only in one half of the line. When these breaches occur, it is because I prefer to let the natural 'sound of sense' prevail over the demands of the convention: I have been reluctant to force an artificial shape or an unusual word choice just for the sake of correctness.

In general, the alliteration varies from the shadowy to the substantial, from the properly to the improperly distributed. Substantial and proper are such lines as

The *fó*rtunes of *wá*r   *fá*voured Hróthgar (line 64)

the *hí*ghest in the *lá*nd,   would *lé*nd advíce (line 172)

and *fí*nd *frí*endship   in the *Fá*ther's embráce (line 188)

Here the caesura is definite, there are two stresses in each half of the line and the first stressed syllable of the second half alliterates with the first or the second or both of the stressed syllables in the first half. The main deviation from this is one that other translators have allowed themselves – the freedom, that is, to alliterate on the fourth stressed syllable, a practice that breaks the rule but that nevertheless does bind the line together:

> We have héard of those prínces' heróic campáigns
> (line 3)

> and he cróssed óver into the Lórd's kéeping (line 27)

In the course of the translation, such deviations, distortions, syncopations and extensions do occur; what I was after first and foremost was a narrative line that sounded as if it meant business and I was prepared to sacrifice other things in pursuit of this directness of utterance.

The appositional nature of the Old English syntax, for example, is somewhat slighted here, as is the *Beowulf* poet's resourcefulness with synonyms and (to a lesser extent) his genius for compound-making, kennings and all sorts of variation. Usually – as at line 1209, where I render *ȳða ful* as 'frothing wave-vat', and at line 1523, where *beado-lēoma* becomes 'battle-torch' – I try to match the poet's analogy-seeking habit at its most original; and I use all the common coinages for the lord of the nation, variously referred to as 'ring-giver', 'treasure-giver', 'his people's shield' or 'shepherd' or 'helmet'. I have been less faithful, however, to the way the poet rings the changes when it comes to compounds meaning a sword or a spear, or a battle or any bloody encounter with foes. Old English abounds in vigorous, evocative and specifically poetic words for these things, but I have tended to follow modern usage and in the main have called a sword a sword.

There was one area, however, where a certain strangeness in the diction came naturally. In those instances where a local Ulster word seemed either poetically or historically right, I felt free to use it. For example, at lines 324 and 2988 I use the word 'graith' for 'harness', and at 3026 'hoked' for 'rooted about', because the local term seemed in each case to have special body and force. Then, for reasons of historical suggestiveness, I have in several instances used the word 'bawn' to refer to Hrothgar's hall. In Elizabethan English, bawn (from the Irish *bó-dhún*, a fort for cattle) referred specifically to the fortified dwellings that the English planters built in Ireland to keep the dispossessed natives at bay, so it seemed the proper term to apply to the embattled keep where Hrothgar waits and watches. Indeed, every time I read the lovely interlude that tells of the minstrel singing in Heorot just before the first attacks of Grendel, I cannot help thinking of Edmund Spenser in Kilcolman Castle, reading the early cantos of *The Faerie Queene* to Sir Walter Raleigh, just before the Irish would burn the castle and drive Spenser out of Munster back to the Elizabethan court. Putting a bawn into *Beowulf* seems one way for an Irish poet to come to terms with that complex history of conquest and colony, absorption and resistance, integrity and antagonism, a history that has to be clearly acknowledged by all concerned in order to render it ever more 'willable forward / again and again and again'.

(Line numbers given above refer to this translation, not to the Anglo-Saxon text.)

Beowulf

Hwæt wē Gār-Dena   in geārdagum,
þēodcyninga   þrym gefrūnon,
hū ðā æþelingas   ellen fremedon.

 Oft Scyld Scēfing   sceaþena þrēatum,
monegum mægþum   meodosetla oftēah,
egsode eorl[as],   syððan ǣrest wearð
fēasceaft funden;   hē þæs frōfre gebād,
wēox under wolcnum,   weorðmyndum þāh,
oðþæt him ǣghwylc þ[ǣr]   ymbsittendra
ofer hronrāde   hȳran scolde,
gomban gyldan.   Þæt wæs gōd cyning!

Ðǣm eafera wæs   æfter cenned
geong in geardum,   þone God sende
folce tō frōfre;   fyrenðearfe ongeat,
þ[e] hīe ǣr drugon   aldor[lē]ase
lange hwīle.   Him þæs Līffrēa,
wuldres Wealdend   woroldāre forgeaf;
Bēowulf wæs brēme   —blǣd wīde sprang—
Scyldes eafera   Scedelandum in.
Swā sceal [geong g]uma   gōde gewyrcean,
fromum feohgiftum   on fæder [bea]rme,
þæt hine on ylde   eft gewunigen
wilgesīþas   þonne wīg cume,
lēode gelǣsten; lofdǣdum sceal
in mǣgþa gehwǣre   man geþēon.

 Him ðā Scyld gewāt   tō gescæphwile,
felahror fēran   on Frēan wǣre.
Hī hyne þā ætbǣron   tō brimes faroðe,
swǣse gesīþas,   swā hē selfa bæd,

So. The Spear-Danes in days gone by
and the kings who ruled them had courage and greatness.
We have heard of those princes' heroic campaigns.

There was Shield Sheafson, scourge of many tribes,
a wrecker of mead-benches, rampaging among foes.
This terror of the hall-troops had come far.
A foundling to start with, he would flourish later on
as his powers waxed and his worth was proved.
In the end each clan on the outlying coasts
beyond the whale-road had to yield to him
and begin to pay tribute. That was one good king.

Afterwards a boy-child was born to Shield,
a cub in the yard, a comfort sent
by God to that nation. He knew what they had tholed,
the long times and troubles they'd come through
without a leader; so the Lord of Life,
the glorious Almighty, made this man renowned.
Shield had fathered a famous son:
Beow's name was known through the north.
And a young prince must be prudent like that,
giving freely while his father lives
so that afterwards in age when fighting starts
steadfast companions will stand by him
and hold the line. Behaviour that's admired
is the path to power among people everywhere.

Shield was still thriving when his time came
and he crossed over into the Lord's keeping.
His warrior band did what he bade them
when he laid down the law among the Danes:

The Danes have
legends about their
warrior kings. The
most famous was
Shield Sheafson,
who founded the
ruling house.

Shield's funeral.

they shouldered him out to the sea's flood,
the chief they revered who had long ruled them.
A ring-whorled prow rode in the harbour,
ice-clad, outbound, a craft for a prince.
They stretched their beloved lord in his boat,
laid out by the mast, amidships,
the great ring-giver. Far-fetched treasures
were piled upon him, and precious gear.
I never heard before of a ship so well furbished
with battle-tackle, bladed weapons
and coats of mail. The massed treasure
was loaded on top of him: it would travel far
on out into the ocean's sway.
They decked his body no less bountifully
with offerings than those first ones did
who cast him away when he was a child
and launched him alone out over the waves.
And they set a gold standard up
high above his head and let him drift
to wind and tide, bewailing him
and mourning their loss. No man can tell,
no wise man in hall or weathered veteran
knows for certain who salvaged that load.

Shield's heirs:
his son Beow
succeeded by
Halfdane,
Halfdane by
Hrothgar.

Then it fell to Beow to keep the forts.
He was well regarded and ruled the Danes
for a long time after his father took leave
of his life on earth. And then his heir,
the great Halfdane, held sway
for as long as he lived, their elder and warlord.
He was four times a father, this fighter prince:
one by one they entered the world,
Heorogar, Hrothgar, the good Halga
and a daughter, I have heard, who was Onela's queen,
a balm in bed for the battle-scarred Swede.

4

The fortunes of war favoured Hrothgar.
Friends and kinsmen flocked to his ranks,
young followers, a force that grew
to a mighty army. So his mind turned
to hall-building: he handed down orders
for men to work on a great mead-hall
meant to be a wonder of the world for ever;
it would be his throne-room and there he would dispense
his God-given goods to young and old –
but not the common land or people's lives.
Far and wide through the world, I have heard,
orders for work to adorn that wallstead
were sent to many peoples. And soon it stood there,
finished and ready, in full view,
the hall of halls. Heorot was the name
he had settled on it, whose utterance was law.
Nor did he renege, but doled out rings
and torques at the table. The hall towered,
its gables wide and high and awaiting
a barbarous burning. That doom abided,
but in time it would come: the killer instinct
unleashed among in-laws, the blood-lust rampant.

Then a powerful demon, a prowler through the dark,
nursed a hard grievance. It harrowed him
to hear the din of the loud banquet
every day in the hall, the harp being struck
and the clear song of a skilled poet
telling with mastery of man's beginnings,
how the Almighty had made the earth
a gleaming plain girdled with waters;
in His splendour He set the sun and the moon
to be earth's lamplight, lanterns for men,
and filled the broad lap of the world
with branches and leaves; and quickened life
in every other thing that moved.

King Hrothgar
builds Heorot Hall.

Heorot is
threatened.

Grendel, a monster descended from 'Cain's clan', begins to prowl. So times were pleasant for the people there
until finally one, a fiend out of hell,
began to work his evil in the world.
Grendel was the name of this grim demon
haunting the marches, marauding round the heath
and the desolate fens; he had dwelt for a time
in misery among the banished monsters,
Cain's clan, whom the Creator had outlawed
and condemned as outcasts. For the killing of Abel
the Eternal Lord had exacted a price:
Cain got no good from committing that murder
because the Almighty made him anathema
and out of the curse of his exile there sprang
ogres and elves and evil phantoms
and the giants too who strove with God
time and again until He gave them their reward.

Grendel attacks Heorot. So, after nightfall, Grendel set out
for the lofty house, to see how the Ring-Danes
were settling into it after their drink,
and there he came upon them, a company of the best
asleep from their feasting, insensible to pain
and human sorrow. Suddenly then
the God-cursed brute was creating havoc:
greedy and grim, he grabbed thirty men
from their resting places and rushed to his lair,
flushed up and inflamed from the raid,
blundering back with the butchered corpses.

Then as dawn brightened and the day broke
Grendel's powers of destruction were plain:
their wassail was over, they wept to heaven
and mourned under morning. Their mighty prince,
the storied leader, sat stricken and helpless,
humiliated by the loss of his guard,

6   [99–131]

bewildered and stunned, staring aghast
at the demon's trail, in deep distress.
He was numb with grief, but got no respite
for one night later merciless Grendel
struck again with more gruesome murders.
Malignant by nature, he never showed remorse.
It was easy then to meet with a man
shifting himself to a safer distance
to bed in the bothies, for who could be blind
to the evidence of his eyes, the obviousness
of that hall-watcher's hate? Whoever escaped
kept a weather-eye open and moved away.

So Grendel ruled in defiance of right,
one against all, until the greatest house
in the world stood empty, a deserted wallstead.
For twelve winters, seasons of woe,
the lord of the Shieldings suffered under
his load of sorrow; and so, before long,
the news was known over the whole world.
Sad lays were sung about the beset king,
the vicious raids and ravages of Grendel,
his long and unrelenting feud,
nothing but war; how he would never
parley or make peace with any Dane
nor stop his death-dealing nor pay the death-price.
No counsellor could ever expect
fair reparation from those rabid hands. ·
All were endangered; young and old
were hunted down by that dark death-shadow
who lurked and swooped in the long nights
on the misty moors; nobody knows
where these reavers from hell roam on their errands.

So Grendel waged his lonely war,
inflicting constant cruelties on the people,

King Hrothgar's
distress and
helplessness.

atrocious hurt. He took over Heorot,
haunted the glittering hall after dark,
but the throne itself, the treasure-seat,
he was kept from approaching; he was the Lord's outcast.

The Danes, hard-pressed, turn for help to heathen gods.

These were hard times, heart-breaking
for the prince of the Shieldings; powerful counsellors,
the highest in the land, would lend advice,
plotting how best the bold defenders
might resist and beat off sudden attacks.
Sometimes at pagan shrines they vowed
offerings to idols, swore oaths
that the killer of souls might come to their aid
and save the people. That was their way,
their heathenish hope; deep in their hearts
they remembered hell. The Almighty Judge
of good deeds and bad, the Lord God,
Head of the Heavens and High King of the World,
was unknown to them. Oh, cursed is he
who in time of trouble has to thrust his soul
in the fire's embrace, forfeiting help;
he has nowhere to turn. But blessed is he
who after death can approach the Lord
and find friendship in the Father's embrace.

So that troubled time continued, woe
that never stopped, steady affliction
for Halfdane's son, too hard an ordeal.
There was panic after dark, people endured
raids in the night, riven by the terror.

At the court of King Hygelac, a Geat warrior prepares to help Hrothgar.

When he heard about Grendel, Hygelac's thane
was on home ground, over in Geatland.
There was no one else like him alive.
In his day, he was the mightiest man on earth,
high-born and powerful. He ordered a boat

8   [132–165]

that would ply the waves. He announced his plan:
to sail the swan's road and search out that king,
the famous prince who needed defenders.
Nobody tried to keep him from going,
no elder denied him, dear as he was to them.
Instead, they inspected omens and spurred
his ambition to go, whilst he moved about
like the leader he was, enlisting men,
the best he could find; with fourteen others
the warrior boarded the boat as captain,
a canny pilot along coast and currents.

Time went by, the boat was on water,
in close under the cliffs.

The hero and his troop sail from the land of the Geats.

Men climbed eagerly up the gangplank,
sand churned in surf, warriors loaded
a cargo of weapons, shining war-gear
in the vessel's hold, then heaved out,
away with a will in their wood-wreathed ship.
Over the waves, with the wind behind her
and foam at her neck, she flew like a bird
until her curved prow had covered the distance
and on the following day, at the due hour,
those seafarers sighted land,
sunlit cliffs, sheer crags
and looming headlands, the landfall they sought.
It was the end of their voyage and the Geats vaulted
over the side, out on to the sand,
and moored their ship. There was a clash of mail
and a thresh of gear. They thanked God
for that easy crossing on a calm sea.

When the watchman on the wall, the Shieldings' lookout
whose job it was to guard the sea-cliffs,
saw shields glittering on the gangplank
and battle-equipment being unloaded

The Danish coastguard challenges the outsiders.

he had to find out who and what
the arrivals were. So he rode to the shore,
this horseman of Hrothgar's, and challenged them
in formal terms, flourishing his spear:

'What kind of men are you who arrive
rigged out for combat in coats of mail,
sailing here over the sea-lanes
in your steep-hulled boat? I have been stationed
as lookout on this coast for a long time.
My job is to watch the waves for raiders,
any danger to the Danish shore.
Never before has a force under arms
disembarked so openly – not bothering to ask
if the sentries allowed them safe passage
or the clan had consented. Nor have I seen
a mightier man-at-arms on this earth
than the one standing here: unless I am mistaken,
he is truly noble. This is no mere
hanger-on in a hero's armour.
So now, before you fare inland
as interlopers, I have to be informed
about who you are and where you hail from.
Outsiders from across the water,
I say it again: the sooner you tell
where you come from and why, the better.'

The Geat hero announces himself and explains his mission.

The leader of the troop unlocked his word-hoard;
the distinguished one delivered this answer:
'We belong by birth to the Geat people
and owe allegiance to Lord Hygelac.
In his day, my father was a famous man,
a noble warrior-lord named Ecgtheow.
He outlasted many a long winter
and went on his way. All over the world
men wise in counsel continue to remember him.

We come in good faith to find your lord
and nation's shield, the son of Halfdane.
Give us the right advice and direction.
We have arrived here on a great errand
to the lord of the Danes, and I believe therefore
there should be nothing hidden or withheld between us.
So tell us if what we have heard is true
about this threat, whatever it is,
this danger abroad in the dark nights,
this corpse-maker mongering death
in the Shieldings' country. I come to proffer
my wholehearted help and counsel.
I can show the wise Hrothgar a way
to defeat his enemy and find respite –
if any respite is to reach him, ever.
I can calm the turmoil and terror in his mind.
Otherwise, he must endure woes
and live with grief for as long as his hall
stands at the horizon, on its high ground.'

Undaunted, sitting astride his horse,
the coast-guard answered, 'Anyone with gumption
and a sharp mind will take the measure
of two things: what's said and what's done.
I believe what you have told me: that you are a troop
loyal to our king. So come ahead
with your arms and your gear, and I will guide you.
What's more, I'll order my own comrades
on their word of honour to watch your boat
down there on the strand – keep her safe
in her fresh tar, until the time comes
for her curved prow to preen on the waves
and bear this hero back to Geatland.
May one so valiant and venturesome
come unharmed through the clash of battle.'

The coastguard
allows the Geats to
pass.

So they went on their way. The ship rode the water,
broad-beamed, bound by its hawser
and anchored fast. Boar-shapes flashed
above their cheek-guards, the brightly forged
work of goldsmiths, watching over
those stern-faced men. They marched in step,
hurrying on till the timbered hall
rose before them, radiant with gold.
Nobody on earth knew of another
building like it. Majesty lodged there,
its light shone over many lands.
So their gallant escort guided them
to that dazzling stronghold and indicated
the shortest way to it; then the noble warrior
wheeled on his horse and spoke these words:
'It is time for me to go. May the Almighty
Father keep you and in His kindness
watch over your exploits. I'm away to the sea,
back on alert against enemy raiders.'

They arrive at
Heorot.

It was a paved track, a path that kept them
in marching order. Their mail-shirts glinted,
hard and hand-linked; the high-gloss iron
of their armour rang. So they duly arrived
in their grim war-graith and gear at the hall,
and, weary from the sea, stacked wide shields
of the toughest hardwood against the wall,
then collapsed on the benches; battle-dress
and weapons clashed. They collected their spears
in a seafarers' stook, a stand of greyish
tapering ash. And the troops themselves
were as good as their weapons.
                                    Then a proud warrior
questioned the men concerning their origins:
'Where do you come from, carrying these
decorated shields and shirts of mail,

12

these cheek-hinged helmets and javelins?
I am Hrothgar's herald and officer.
I have never seen so impressive or large
an assembly of strangers. Stoutness of heart,
bravery not banishment, must have brought you to Hrothgar.'

The man whose name was known for courage,
the Geat leader, resolute in his helmet,
answered in return: 'We are retainers
from Hygelac's band. Beowulf is my name.
If your lord and master, the most renowned
son of Halfdane, will hear me out
and graciously allow me to greet him in person,
I am ready and willing to report my errand.'

Beowulf announces
his name.

Wulfgar replied, a Wendel chief
renowned as a warrior, well known for his wisdom
and the temper of his mind: 'I will take this message,
in accordance with your wish, to our noble king,
our dear lord, friend of the Danes,
the giver of rings. I will go and ask him
about your coming here, then hurry back
with whatever reply it pleases him to give.'

Formalities are
observed.

With that he turned to where Hrothgar sat,
an old man among retainers;
the valiant follower stood foursquare
in front of his king: he knew the courtesies.
Wulfgar addressed his dear lord:
'People from Geatland have put ashore.
They have sailed far over the wide sea.
They call the chief in charge of their band
by the name of Beowulf. They beg, my lord,
an audience with you, exchange of words
and formal greeting. Most gracious Hrothgar,
do not refuse them, but grant them a reply.

From their arms and appointment, they appear well born
and worthy of respect, especially the one
who has led them this far: he is formidable indeed.'

Hrothgar recog-
nizes Beowulf's
name and approves
his arrival. Hrothgar, protector of Shieldings, replied:
'I used to know him when he was a young boy.
His father before him was called Ecgtheow.
Hrethel the Geat gave Ecgtheow
his daughter in marriage. This man is their son,
here to follow up an old friendship.
A crew of seamen who sailed for me once
with a gift-cargo across to Geatland
returned with marvellous tales about him:
a thane, they declared, with the strength of thirty
in the grip of each hand. Now Holy God
has, in His goodness, guided him here
to the West-Danes, to defend us from Grendel.
This is my hope; and for his heroism
I will recompense him with a rich treasure.
Go immediately, bid him and the Geats
he has in attendance to assemble and enter.
Say, moreover, when you speak to them,
they are welcome to Denmark.'

At the door of the hall,

Wulfgar duly delivered the message:
'My lord, the conquering king of the Danes,
bids me announce that he knows your ancestry;
also that he welcomes you here to Heorot
and salutes your arrival from across the sea.
You are free now to move forward
to meet Hrothgar, in helmets and armour,
but shields must stay here and spears be stacked
until the outcome of the audience is clear.'

Beowulf enters
Heorot. The hero arose, surrounded closely
by his powerful thanes. A party remained

14   [368–400]

under orders to keep watch on the arms;
the rest proceeded, led by their prince
under Heorot's roof. And standing on the hearth
in webbed links that the smith had woven,
the fine-forged mesh of his gleaming mail-shirt,
resolute in his helmet, Beowulf spoke:
'Greetings to Hrothgar. I am Hygelac's kinsman,
one of his hall-troop. When I was younger,
I had great triumphs. Then news of Grendel,
hard to ignore, reached me at home:
sailors brought stories of the plight you suffer
in this legendary hall, how it lies deserted,
empty and useless once the evening light
hides itself under heaven's dome.
So every elder and experienced councilman
among my people supported my resolve
to come here to you, King Hrothgar,
because all knew of my awesome strength.
They had seen me boltered in the blood of enemies
when I battled and bound five beasts,
raided a troll-nest and in the night-sea
slaughtered sea-brutes. I have suffered extremes
and avenged the Geats (their enemies brought it
upon themselves, I devastated them).
Now I mean to be a match for Grendel,
settle the outcome in single combat.
And so, my request, O king of Bright-Danes,
dear prince of the Shieldings, friend of the people
and their ring of defence, my one request
is that you won't refuse me, who have come this far,
the privilege of purifying Heorot,
with my own men to help me, and nobody else.
I have heard moreover that the monster scorns
in his reckless way to use weapons;
therefore, to heighten Hygelac's fame
and gladden his heart, I hereby renounce

He gives an account
of his heroic
exploits.

sword and the shelter of the broad shield,
the heavy war-board: hand-to-hand
is how it will be, a life-and-death
fight with the fiend. Whichever one death fells
must deem it a just judgement by God.
If Grendel wins, it will be a gruesome day;
he will glut himself on the Geats in the war-hall,
swoop without fear on that flower of manhood
as on others before. Then my face won't be there
to be covered in death: he will carry me away
as he goes to ground, gorged and bloodied;
he will run gloating with my raw corpse
and feed on it alone, in a cruel frenzy,
fouling his moor-nest. No need then
to lament for long or lay out my body:
if the battle takes me send back
this breast-webbing that Weland fashioned
and Hrethel gave me to Lord Hygelac.
Fate goes ever as fate must.'

Hrothgar recollects a friendship and tells of Grendel's raids.

Hrothgar, the helmet of Shieldings, spoke:
'Beowulf, my friend, you have travelled here
to favour us with help and to fight for us.
There was a feud one time, begun by your father.
With his own hands he had killed Heatholaf,
who was a Wulfing; so war was looming
and his people, in fear of it, forced him to leave.
He came away then over rolling waves
to the South-Danes here, the sons of honour.
I was then in the first flush of kingship,
establishing my sway over the rich strongholds
of this heroic land. Heorogar,
my older brother and the better man,
also a son of Halfdane's, had died.
Finally I healed the feud by paying:
I shipped a treasure-trove to the Wulfings

16

and Ecgtheow acknowledged me with oaths of allegiance.

'It bothers me to have to burden anyone
with all the grief Grendel has caused
and the havoc he has wreaked upon us in Heorot,
our humiliations. My household-guard
are on the wane, fate sweeps them away
into Grendel's clutches –
                                    but God can easily
halt these raids and harrowing attacks!

'Time and again, when the goblets passed
and seasoned fighters got flushed with beer,
they would pledge themselves to protect Heorot
and wait for Grendel with whetted swords.
But when dawn broke and day crept in
over each empty, blood-spattered bench,
the floor of the mead-hall where they had feasted
would be slick with slaughter. And so they died,
faithful retainers, and my following dwindled.

'Now take your place at the table, relish
the triumph of heroes to your heart's content.'

Then a bench was cleared in that banquet hall   A feast in Heorot.
so the Geats could have room to be together
and the party sat, proud in their bearing,
strong and stalwart. An attendant stood by
with a decorated pitcher, pouring bright
helpings of mead. And the minstrel sang,
filling Heorot with his head-clearing voice,
gladdening that great rally of Geats and Danes.

From where he crouched at the king's feet,   Unferth strikes a
Unferth, a son of Ecglaf's, spoke   discordant note.
contrary words. Beowulf's coming,

his sea-braving, made him sick with envy:
he could not brook or abide the fact
that anyone else alive under heaven
might enjoy greater regard than he did:

Unferth's version
of a swimming
contest.

'Are you the Beowulf who took on Breca
in a swimming match on the open sea,
risking the water just to prove that you could win?
It was sheer vanity made you venture out
on the main deep. And no matter who tried,
friend or foe, to deflect the pair of you,
neither would back down: the sea-test obsessed you.
You waded in, embracing water,
taking its measure, mastering currents,
riding on the swell. The ocean swayed,
winter went wild in the waves, but you vied
for seven nights; and then he outswam you,
came ashore the stronger contender.
He was cast up safe and sound one morning
among the Heathoreams, then made his way
to where he belonged in Bronding country,
home again, sure of his ground
in strongroom and bawn. So Breca made good
his boast upon you and was proved right.
No matter, therefore, how you may have fared
in every bout and battle until now,
this time you'll be worsted; no one has ever
outlasted an entire night against Grendel.'

Beowulf corrects
Unferth.

Beowulf, Ecgtheow's son, replied:
'Well, friend Unferth, you have had your say
about Breca and me. But it was mostly beer
that was doing the talking. The truth is this:
when the going was heavy in those high waves,
I was the strongest swimmer of all.
We'd been children together and we grew up
daring ourselves to outdo each other,

18   [502–36]

boasting and urging each other to risk
our lives on the sea. And so it turned out.
Each of us swam holding a sword,
a naked, hard-proofed blade for protection
against the whale-beasts. But Breca could never
move out farther or faster from me
than I could manage to move from him.
Shoulder to shoulder, we struggled on
for five nights, until the long flow
and pitch of the waves, the perishing cold,
night falling and winds from the north
drove us apart. The deep boiled up
and its wallowing sent the sea-brutes wild.
My armour helped me to hold out;
my hard-ringed chain-mail, hand-forged and linked,
a fine, close-fitting filigree of gold,
kept me safe when some ocean creature
pulled me to the bottom. Pinioned fast
and swathed in its grip, I was granted one
final chance: my sword plunged
and the ordeal was over. Through my own hands,
the fury of battle had finished off the sea-beast.

'Time and again, foul things attacked me,
lurking and stalking, but I lashed out,
gave as good as I got with my sword.
My flesh was not for feasting on,
there would be no monsters gnawing and gloating
over their banquet at the bottom of the sea.
Instead, in the morning, mangled and sleeping
the sleep of the sword, they slopped and floated
like the ocean's leavings. From now on
sailors would be safe, the deep-sea raids
were over for good. Light came from the east,
bright guarantee of God, and the waves
went quiet; I could see headlands

Beowulf survives his
ordeal in the sea.

and buffeted cliffs. Often, for undaunted courage,
fate spares the man it has not already marked.
However it occurred, my sword had killed
nine sea-monsters. Such night-dangers
and hard ordeals I have never heard of
nor of a man more desolate in surging waves.
But worn out as I was, I survived,
came through with my life. The ocean lifted
and laid me ashore, I landed safe
on the coast of Finland.

Unferth rebuked.
Beowulf reaffirms
his determination
to defeat Grendel.

                           Now I cannot recall
any fight you entered, Unferth,
that bears comparison. I don't boast when I say
that neither you nor Breca were ever much
celebrated for swordsmanship
or for facing danger on the field of battle.
You killed your own kith and kin,
so for all your cleverness and quick tongue,
you will suffer damnation in the depths of hell.
The fact is, Unferth, if you were truly
as keen or courageous as you claim to be
Grendel would never have got away with
such unchecked atrocity, attacks on your king,
havoc in Heorot and horrors everywhere.
But he knows he need never be in dread
of your blade making a mizzle of his blood
or of vengeance arriving ever from this quarter –
from the Victory-Shieldings, the shoulderers of the spear.
He knows he can trample down you Danes
to his heart's content, humiliate and murder
without fear of reprisal. But he will find me different.
I will show him how Geats shape to kill
in the heat of battle. Then whoever wants to
may go bravely to mead, when morning light,
scarfed in sun-dazzle, shines forth from the south
and brings another daybreak to the world.'

Then the grey-haired treasure-giver was glad;
far-famed in battle, the prince of Bright-Danes
and keeper of his people counted on Beowulf,
on the warrior's steadfastness and his word.
So the laughter started, the din got louder
and the crowd was happy. Wealhtheow came in,
Hrothgar's queen, observing the courtesies.
Adorned in her gold, she graciously saluted
the men in hall, then handed the cup
first to Hrothgar, their homeland's guardian,
urging him to drink deep and enjoy it
because he was dear to them. And he drank it down
like the warlord he was, with festive cheer.
So the Helming woman went on her rounds,
queenly and dignified, decked out in rings,
offering the goblet to all ranks,
treating the household and the assembled troop
until it was Beowulf's turn to take it from her hand.
With measured words she welcomed the Geat
and thanked God for granting her wish
that a deliverer she could believe in would arrive
to ease their afflictions. He accepted the cup,
a daunting man, dangerous in action
and eager for it always. He addressed Wealhtheow;
Beowulf, son of Ecgtheow, said:

'I had a fixed purpose when I put to sea.
As I sat in the boat with my band of men,
I meant to perform to the uttermost
what your people wanted or perish in the attempt,
in the fiend's clutches. And I shall fulfil that purpose,
prove myself with a proud deed
or meet my death here in the mead-hall.'

This formal boast by Beowulf the Geat
pleased the lady well and she went to sit

Wealhtheow,
Hrothgar's queen,
graces the banquet.

Beowulf's formal
boast.

by Hrothgar, regal and arrayed with gold.

Hrothgar leaves
Heorot in
Beowulf's keeping. Then it was like old times in the echoing hall,
proud talk and the people happy,
loud and excited; until soon enough
Halfdane's heir had to be away
to his night's rest. He realized
that the demon was going to descend on the hall,
that he had plotted all day, from dawn-light
until darkness gathered again over the world
and stealthy night-shapes came stealing forth
under the cloud-murk. The company stood
as the two leaders took leave of each other:
Hrothgar wished Beowulf health and good luck,
named him hall-warden and announced as follows:
'Never, since my hand could hold a shield
have I entrusted or given control
of the Danes' hall to anyone but you.
Ward and guard it, for it is the greatest of houses.
Be on your mettle now, keep in mind your fame,
beware of the enemy. There's nothing you wish for
that won't be yours if you win through alive.'

Hrothgar departed then with his house-guard.
The lord of the Shieldings, their shelter in war,
left the mead-hall to lie with Wealhtheow,
his queen and bedmate. The King of Glory
(as people learned) had posted a lookout
who was a match for Grendel, a guard against monsters,
special protection to the Danish prince.
And the Geat placed complete trust
in his strength of limb and the Lord's favour.
He began to remove his iron breast-mail,
took off the helmet and handed his attendant
the patterned sword, a smith's masterpiece,
ordering him to keep the equipment guarded.

And before he bedded down, Beowulf,
that prince of goodness, proudly asserted:
'When it comes to fighting, I count myself
as dangerous any day as Grendel.
So it won't be a cutting edge I'll wield
to mow him down, easily as I might.
He has no idea of the arts of war,
of shield or sword-play, although he does possess
a wild strength. No weapons, therefore,
for either this night: unarmed he shall face me
if face me he dares. And may the Divine Lord
in His wisdom grant the glory of victory
to whichever side He sees fit.'

Beowulf renounces
the use of weapons.

Then down the brave man lay with his bolster
under his head and his whole company
of sea-rovers at rest beside him.
None of them expected he would ever see
his homeland again or get back
to his native place and the people who reared him.
They knew too well the way it was before,
how often the Danes had fallen prey
to death in the mead-hall. But the Lord was weaving
a victory on his war-loom for the Weather-Geats.
Through the strength of one they all prevailed;
they would crush their enemy and come through
in triumph and gladness. The truth is clear:
Almighty God rules over mankind
and always has.
              Then out of the night
came the shadow-stalker, stealthy and swift;
the hall-guards were slack, asleep at their posts,
all except one; it was widely understood
that as long as God disallowed it,
the fiend could not bear them to his shadow-bourne.
One man, however, was in fighting mood,

The Geats await
Grendel's attack.

awake and on edge, spoiling for action.

Grendel strikes. In off the moors, down through the mist-bands
God-cursed Grendel came greedily loping.
The bane of the race of men roamed forth,
hunting for a prey in the high hall.
Under the cloud-murk he moved towards it
until it shone above him, a sheer keep
of fortified gold. Nor was that the first time
he had scouted the grounds of Hrothgar's dwelling –
although never in his life, before or since,
did he find harder fortune or hall-defenders.
Spurned and joyless, he journeyed on ahead
and arrived at the bawn. The iron-braced door
turned on its hinge when his hands touched it.
Then his rage boiled over, he ripped open
the mouth of the building, maddening for blood,
pacing the length of the patterned floor
with his loathsome tread, while a baleful light,
flame more than light, flared from his eyes.
He saw many men in the mansion, sleeping,
a ranked company of kinsmen and warriors
quartered together. And his glee was demonic,
picturing the mayhem: before morning
he would rip life from limb and devour them,
feed on their flesh; but his fate that night
was due to change, his days of ravening
had come to an end.
A Geat warrior
perishes.   Mighty and canny,
Hygelac's kinsman was keenly watching
for the first move the monster would make.
Nor did the creature keep him waiting
but struck suddenly and started in;
he grabbed and mauled a man on his bench,
bit into his bone-lappings, bolted down his blood
and gorged on him in lumps, leaving the body

utterly lifeless, eaten up
hand and foot. Venturing closer,
his talon was raised to attack Beowulf
where he lay on the bed, he was bearing in
with open claw when the alert hero's
comeback and armlock forestalled him utterly.
The captain of evil discovered himself
in a handgrip harder than anything
he had ever encountered in any man
on the face of the earth. Every bone in his body
quailed and recoiled, but he could not escape.
He was desperate to flee to his den and hide
with the devil's litter, for in all his days
he had never been clamped or cornered like this.
Then Hygelac's trusty retainer recalled
his bedtime speech, sprang to his feet
and got a firm hold. Fingers were bursting,
the monster back-tracking, the man overpowering.
The dread of the land was desperate to escape,
to take a roundabout road and flee
to his lair in the fens. The latching power
in his fingers weakened; it was the worst trip
the terror-monger had taken to Heorot.
And now the timbers trembled and sang,
a hall-session that harrowed every Dane
inside the stockade: stumbling in fury,
the two contenders crashed through the building.
The hall clattered and hammered, but somehow
survived the onslaught and kept standing:
it was handsomely structured, a sturdy frame
braced with the best of blacksmith's work
inside and out. The story goes
that as the pair struggled, mead-benches were smashed
and sprung off the floor, gold fittings and all.
Before then, no Shielding elder would believe
there was any power or person upon earth

Beowulf's fight with
Grendel.

capable of wrecking their horn-rigged hall
unless the burning embrace of a fire
engulf it in flame. Then an extraordinary
wail arose, and bewildering fear
came over the Danes. Everyone felt it
who heard that cry as it echoed off the wall,
a God-cursed scream and strain of catastrophe,
the howl of the loser, the lament of the hell-serf
keening his wound. He was overwhelmed,
manacled tight by the man who of all men
was foremost and strongest in the days of this life.

Beowulf's thanes
defend him.

But the earl-troop's leader was not inclined
to allow his caller to depart alive:
he did not consider that life of much account
to anyone anywhere. Time and again,
Beowulf's warriors worked to defend
their lord's life, laying about them
as best they could with their ancestral blades.
Stalwart in action, they kept striking out
on every side, seeking to cut
straight to the soul. When they joined the struggle
there was something they could not have known at the time,
that no blade on earth, no blacksmith's art
could ever damage their demon opponent.
He had conjured the harm from the cutting edge
of every weapon. But his going away
out of this world and the days of his life
would be agony to him, and his alien spirit
would travel far into fiends' keeping.

Grendel is defeat-
ed, Beowulf fulfils
his boast.

Then he who had harrowed the hearts of men
with pain and affliction in former times
and had given offence also to God
found that his bodily powers failed him.
Hygelac's kinsman kept him helplessly

26

locked in a handgrip. As long as either lived,
he was hateful to the other. The monster's whole
body was in pain, a tremendous wound
appeared on his shoulder. Sinews split
and the bone-lappings burst. Beowulf was granted
the glory of winning; Grendel was driven
under the fen-banks, fatally hurt,
to his desolate lair. His days were numbered,
the end of his life was coming over him,
he knew it for certain; and one bloody clash
had fulfilled the dearest wishes of the Danes.
The man who had lately landed among them,
proud and sure, had purged the hall,
kept it from harm; he was happy with his nightwork
and the courage he had shown. The Geat captain
had boldly fulfilled his boast to the Danes:
he had healed and relieved a huge distress,
unremitting humiliations,
the hard fate they'd been forced to undergo,
no small affliction. Clear proof of this
could be seen in the hand the hero displayed
high up near the roof: the whole of Grendel's
shoulder and arm, his awesome grasp.

Then morning came and many a warrior
gathered, as I've heard, around the gift-hall,
clan-chiefs flocking from far and near
down wide-ranging roads, wondering greatly
at the monster's footprints. His fatal departure
was regretted by no one who witnessed his trail,
the ignominious marks of his flight
where he'd skulked away, exhausted in spirit
and beaten in battle, bloodying the path,
hauling his doom to the demons' mere.
The bloodshot water wallowed and surged,
there were loathsome upthrows and overturnings

The morning after:
relief and rejoicing.

of waves and gore and wound-slurry.
With his death upon him, he had dived deep
into his marsh-den, drowned out his life
and his heathen soul: hell claimed him there.

Then away they rode, the old retainers
with many a young man following after,
a troop on horseback, in high spirits
on their bay steeds. Beowulf's doings
were praised over and over again.
Nowhere, they said, north or south
between the two seas or under the tall sky
on the broad earth was there anyone better
to raise a shield or to rule a kingdom.
Yet there was no laying of blame on their lord,
the noble Hrothgar; he was a good king.

At times the war-band broke into a gallop,
letting their chestnut horses race
wherever they found the going good

Hrothgar's
minstrel sings
about Beowulf.

on those well-known tracks. Meanwhile, a thane
of the king's household, a carrier of tales,
a traditional singer deeply schooled
in the lore of the past, linked a new theme
to a strict metre. The man started
to recite with skill, rehearsing Beowulf's
triumphs and feats in well-fashioned lines,
entwining his words.

The tale of
Sigemund, the
dragon-slayer.
Appropriate for
Beowulf, who has
defeated Grendel.

                    He told what he'd heard
repeated in songs about Sigemund's exploits,
all of those many feats and marvels,
the struggles and wanderings of Waels's son,
things unknown to anyone
except to Fitela, feuds and foul doings
confided by uncle to nephew when he felt
the urge to speak of them: always they had been

partners in the fight, friends in need.
They killed giants, their conquering swords
had brought them down.

                   After his death
Sigemund's glory   grew and grew
because of his courage   when he killed the dragon,
the guardian of the hoard.   Under grey stone
he had dared to enter   all by himself
to face the worst   without Fitela.
But it came to pass   that his sword plunged
right through   those radiant scales
and drove into the wall.   The dragon died of it.
His daring had given him   total possession
of the treasure-hoard,   his to dispose of
however he liked.   He loaded a boat:
Waels's son   weighted her hold
with dazzling spoils.   The hot dragon melted.

Sigemund's name   was known everywhere.
He was utterly valiant   and venturesome,
a fence round his fighters   and flourished therefore
after King Heremod's   prowess declined
and his campaigns slowed down.   The king was betrayed,
ambushed in Jutland,   overpowered
and done away with.   The waves of his grief
had beaten him down,   made him a burden,
a source of anxiety   to his own nobles:
that expedition   was often condemned
in those earlier times   by experienced men,
men who relied   on his lordship for redress,
who presumed that the part   of a prince was to thrive
on his father's throne   and defend the nation,
the Shielding land   where they lived and belonged,
its holdings and strongholds.   Such was Beowulf
in the affection of his friends   and of everyone alive.
But evil entered   into Heremod.

King Heremod
remembered and
contrasted with
Beowulf.

Meanwhile, the Danes kept racing their mounts
down the sandy lanes. The light of day
broke and kept brightening. Bands of retainers
galloped in excitement to the gabled hall
to see the marvel; and the king himself,
guardian of the ring-hoard, goodness in person,
walked in majesty from the women's quarters
with a numerous train, attended by his queen
and her crowd of maidens, across to the mead-hall.

King Hrothgar
gives thanks for
the relief of
Heorot and adopts
Beowulf 'in his
heart'.
When Hrothgar arrived at the hall, he spoke,
standing on the steps, under the steep eaves,
gazing at the roofwork and Grendel's talon:
'First and foremost, let the Almighty Father
be thanked for this sight. I suffered a long
harrowing by Grendel. But the Heavenly Shepherd
can work His wonders always and everywhere.
Not long since, it seemed I would never
be granted the slightest solace or relief
from any of my burdens: the best of houses
glittered and reeked and ran with blood.
This one worry outweighed all others –
a constant distress to counsellors entrusted
with defending the people's forts from assault
by monsters and demons. But now a man,
with the Lord's assistance, has accomplished something
none of us could manage before now
for all our efforts. Whoever she was
who brought forth this flower of manhood,
if she is still alive, that woman can say
that in her labour the Lord of Ages
bestowed a grace on her. So now, Beowulf,
I adopt you in my heart as a dear son.
Nourish and maintain this new connection,
you noblest of men; there'll be nothing you'll want for,
no worldly goods that won't be yours.

[915–49]

I have often honoured smaller achievements,
recognized warriors not nearly as worthy,
lavished rewards on the less deserving.
But you have made yourself immortal
by your glorious action. May the God of Ages
continue to keep and requite you well.'

Beowulf, son of Ecgtheow, spoke:

'We have gone through with a glorious endeavour
and been much favoured in this fight we dared
against the unknown. Nevertheless,
if you could have seen the monster himself
where he lay beaten, I would have been better pleased.
My plan was to pounce, pin him down
in a tight grip and grapple him to death –
have him panting for life, powerless and clasped
in my bare hands, his body in thrall.
But I couldn't stop him from slipping my hold.
The Lord allowed it, my lock on him
wasn't strong enough, he struggled fiercely
and broke and ran. Yet he bought his freedom
at a high price, for he left his hand
and arm and shoulder to show he had been here,
a cold comfort for having come among us.
And now he won't be long for this world.
He has done his worst but the wound will end him.
He is hasped and hooped and hirpling with pain,
limping and looped in it. Like a man outlawed
for wickedness, he must await
the mighty judgement of God in majesty.'

There was less tampering and big talk then
from Unferth the boaster, less of his blather
as the hall-thanes eyed the awful proof
of the hero's prowess, the splayed hand
up under the eaves. Every nail,

claw-scale and spur, every spike
and welt on the hand of that heathen brute
was like barbed steel. Everybody said
there was no honed iron hard enough
to pierce him through, no time-proofed blade
that could cut his brutal, blood-caked claw.

The damaged hall
repaired. Then the order was given for all hands
to help to refurbish Heorot immediately:
men and women thronging the wine-hall,
getting it ready. Gold thread shone
in the wall-hangings, woven scenes
that attracted and held the eye's attention.
But iron-braced as the inside of it had been,
that bright room lay in ruins now.
The very doors had been dragged from their hinges.
Only the roof remained unscathed
by the time the guilt-fouled fiend turned tail
in despair of his life. But death is not easily
escaped from by anyone:
all of us with souls, earth-dwellers
and children of men, must make our way
to a destination already ordained
where the body, after the banqueting,
sleeps on its deathbed.

A victory feast.   Then the due time arrived
for Halfdane's son to proceed to the hall.
The king himself would sit down to feast.
No group ever gathered in greater numbers
or better order around their ring-giver.
The benches filled with famous men
who fell to with relish; round upon round
of mead was passed; those powerful kinsmen,
Hrothgar and Hrothulf, were in high spirits
in the raftered hall. Inside Heorot
there was nothing but friendship. The Shielding nation

was not yet familiar with feud and betrayal.

Then Halfdane's son presented Beowulf
with a gold standard as a victory gift,
an embroidered banner; also breast-mail
and a helmet; and a sword carried high,
that was both precious object and token of honour.
So Beowulf drank his drink, at ease;
it was hardly a shame to be showered with such gifts
in front of the hall-troops. There haven't been many
moments, I am sure, when men exchanged
four such treasures at so friendly a sitting.
An embossed ridge, a band lapped with wire,
arched over the helmet: head-protection
to keep the keen-ground cutting edge
from damaging it when danger threatened
and the man was battling behind his shield.
Next the king ordered eight horses
with gold bridles to be brought through the yard
into the hall. The harness of one
included a saddle of sumptuous design,
the battle-seat where the son of Halfdane
rode when he wished to join the sword-play –
wherever the killing and carnage were the worst,
he would be to the fore, fighting hard.
Then the Danish prince, descendant of Ing,
handed over both the arms and the horses,
urging Beowulf to use them well.
And so their leader, the lord and guard
of coffer and strongroom, with customary grace
bestowed upon Beowulf both sets of gifts.
A fair witness can see how well each one behaved.

Victory gifts
presented to
Beowulf.

The chieftain went on to reward the others:
each man on the bench who had sailed with Beowulf
and risked the voyage received a bounty,

The other Geats are
rewarded.

some treasured possession. And compensation,
a price in gold, was settled for the Geat
Grendel had cruelly killed earlier –
as he would have killed more, had not mindful God
and one man's daring prevented that doom.
Past and present, God's will prevails.
Hence, understanding is always best
and a prudent mind. Whoever remains
for long here in this earthly life
will enjoy and endure more than enough.

Another lay
performed by the
minstrel.
They sang then and played to please the hero,
words and music for their warrior prince,
harp tunes and tales of adventure:
there were high times on the hall benches
and the king's poet performed his part
with the saga of Finn and his sons, unfolding
the tale of the fierce attack in Friesland
where Hnaef, king of the Danes, met death.

Hildeburh, a
Danish princess
married to the
Frisian King
Finn, loses her son
(unnamed here)
and her brother
Hnaef
in a fight at
Finn's hall.
Hildeburh

had little cause

to credit the Jutes:

son and brother,

she lost them both

on the battlefield.

She, bereft

and blameless, they

foredoomed, cut down

and spear-gored. She,

the woman in shock,

waylaid by grief,

Hoc's daughter –

how could she not

lament her fate

when morning came

34

[1052–77]

and the light broke
           on her murdered dears?
And so farewell
           delight on earth,
war carried away
           Finn's troop of thanes,
all but a few.
           How then could Finn
hold the line
           or fight on
to the end with Hengest,
           how save
the rump of his force
           from that enemy chief?
So a truce was offered
           as follows: first
separate quarters
           to be cleared for the Danes,
hall and throne
           to be shared with the Frisians.
Then, second:
           every day
at the dole-out of gifts
           Finn son of Focwald
should honour the Danes,
           bestow with an even
hand to Hengest
           and Hengest's men
the wrought-gold rings,
           bounty to match
the measure he gave
           his own Frisians –
to keep morale
           in the beer-hall high.
Both sides then
           sealed their agreement.

The Danish attack
is bloody but
indecisive. Hnaef is
killed, Hengest
takes charge and
makes a truce with
Finn and the
Frisians.

The Danish
survivors to be

quartered and
given parity of
treatment with the
Frisians and their
allies, the Jutes.

With oaths to Hengest
                    Finn swore
openly, solemnly,
                    that the battle survivors
would be guaranteed
                    honour and status.
No infringement
                    by word or deed,
no provocation
                    would be permitted.
Their own ring-giver
                    after all
was dead and gone,
                    they were leaderless,
in forced allegiance
                    to his murderer.
So if any Frisian
                    stirred up bad blood
with insinuations
                    or taunts about this,
the blade of the sword
                    would arbitrate it.

The bodies of the
slain burnt on the
pyre.

A funeral pyre
                    was then prepared,
effulgent gold
                    brought out from the hoard.
The pride and prince
                    of the Shieldings lay
awaiting the flame.
                    Everywhere
there were blood-plastered
                    coats of mail.
The pyre was heaped
                    with boar-shaped helmets
forged in gold,
                    with the gashed corpses

of well-born Danes –
                  many had fallen.
Then Hildeburh
                  ordered her own
son's body
                  be burnt with Hnaef's,
the flesh on his bones
                  to sputter and blaze
beside his uncle's.
                  The woman wailed
and sang keens,
                  the warrior went up.
Carcass flame
                  swirled and fumed,
they stood round the burial
                  mound and howled
as heads melted,
                  crusted gashes
spattered and ran
                  bloody matter.
The glutton element
                  flamed and consumed
the dead of both sides.
                  Their great days were gone.
Warriors scattered
                  to homes and forts
all over Friesland,
                  fewer now, feeling
loss of friends.
                  Hengest stayed,
lived out that whole
                  resentful, blood-sullen
winter with Finn,
                  homesick and helpless.
No ring-whorled prow
                  could up then

The Danes,
homesick and
resentful, spend a
winter in exile.

and away on the sea.
                        Wind and water
raged with storms,
                        wave and shingle
were shackled in ice
                        until another year
appeared in the yard
                        as it does to this day,
the seasons constant,
                        the wonder of light
coming over us.

Spring comes.   *Then winter was gone,*
earth's lap grew lovely,
                        longing woke
in the cooped-up exile
                        for a voyage home –
but more for vengeance,
                        some way of bringing
things to a head:
                        his sword arm hankered
to greet the Jutes.
                        So he did not balk
once Hunlafing

Danish warriors
spur themselves to
renew the feud.
Finn is killed, his
stronghold looted,
his widow
Hildeburh carried
back to Denmark.   *placed on his lap*
Dazzle-the-Duel,
                        the best sword of all,
whose edges Jutes
                        knew only too well.
Thus blood was spilled,
                        the gallant Finn
slain in his home
                        after Guthlaf and Oslaf
back from their voyage
                        made old accusation:
the brutal ambush,
                        the fate they had suffered,

all blamed on Finn.
                    The wildness in them
had to brim over.
                    The hall ran red
with blood of enemies.
                    Finn was cut down,
the queen brought away
                    and everything
the Shieldings could find
                    inside Finn's walls –
the Frisian king's
                    gold collars and gemstones –
swept off to the ship.
                    Over sea-lanes then
back to Daneland
                    the warrior troop
bore that lady home.

        The poem was over,
the poet had performed, a pleasant murmur
started on the benches, stewards did the rounds
with wine in splendid jugs, and Wealhtheow came to sit
in her gold crown between two good men,
uncle and nephew, each one of whom
still trusted the other; and the forthright Unferth,
admired by all for his mind and courage
although under a cloud for killing his brothers,
reclined near the king.
                        The queen spoke:
'Enjoy this drink, my most generous lord;
raise up your goblet, entertain the Geats
duly and gently, discourse with them,
be open-handed, happy and fond.
Relish their company, but recollect as well
all of the boons that have been bestowed on you.
The bright court of Heorot has been cleansed

and now the word is that you want to adopt
this warrior as a son. So, while you may,
bask in your fortune, and then bequeath
kingdom and nation to your kith and kin,
before your decease. I am certain of Hrothulf.
He is noble and will use the young ones well.
He will not let you down. Should you die before him,
he will treat our children truly and fairly.
He will honour, I am sure, our two sons,
repay them in kind when he recollects
all the good things we gave him once,
the favour and respect he found in his childhood.'

She turned then to the bench where her boys sat,
Hrethric and Hrothmund, with other nobles' sons,
all the youth together; and that good man,
Beowulf the Geat, sat between the brothers.

Gifts presented, The cup was carried to him, kind words
including a torque: spoken in welcome and a wealth of wrought gold
Beowulf will
present it in due graciously bestowed: two arm-bangles,
course to King a mail-shirt and rings, and the most resplendent
Hygelac, who will torque of gold I ever heard tell of
die wearing it. anywhere on earth or under heaven.
There was no hoard like it since Hama snatched
the Brosings' neck-chain and bore it away
with its gems and settings to his shining fort,
away from Eormenric's wiles and hatred,
and thereby ensured his eternal reward.
Hygelac the Geat, grandson of Swerting,
wore this neck-ring on his last raid;
at bay under his banner, he defended the booty,
treasure he had won. Fate swept him away
because of his proud need to provoke
a feud with the Frisians. He fell beneath his shield,
in the same gem-crusted, kingly gear

[1176–209]

he had worn when he crossed the frothing wave-vat.
So the dead king fell into Frankish hands.
They took his breast-mail, also his neck-torque,
and punier warriors plundered the slain
when the carnage ended; Geat corpses
covered the field.
                  Applause filled the hall.
Then Wealhtheow pronounced in the presence of the
   company:
'Take delight in this torque, dear Beowulf,
wear it for luck and wear also this mail
from our people's armoury: may you prosper in them!
Be acclaimed for strength, for kindly guidance
to these two boys, and your bounty will be sure.
You have won renown: you are known to all men
far and near, now and forever.
Your sway is wide as the wind's home,
as the sea around cliffs. And so, my prince,
I wish you a lifetime's luck and blessings
to enjoy this treasure. Treat my sons
with tender care, be strong and kind.
Here each comrade is true to the other,
loyal to lord, loving in spirit.
The thanes have one purpose, the people are ready:
having drunk and pledged, the ranks do as I bid.'

She moved then to her place. Men were drinking wine   Bedtime in Heorot.
at that rare feast; how could they know fate,
the grim shape of things to come,
the threat looming over many thanes
as night approached and King Hrothgar prepared
to retire to his quarters? Retainers in great numbers
were posted on guard as so often in the past.
Benches were pushed back, bedding-gear and bolsters
spread across the floor, and one man
lay down to his rest, already marked for death.

At their heads they placed their polished timber
battle-shields; and on the bench over them,
each man's kit was kept to hand:
a towering war-helmet, webbed mail-shirt
and great-shafted spear. It was their habit
always and everywhere to be ready for action,
at home or in the camp, in whatever case
and at whatever time the need arose
to rally round their lord. They were a right people.

Another threat is
lurking in the
night. They went to sleep. And one paid dearly
for his night's ease, as had happened to them often,
ever since Grendel occupied the gold-hall,
committing evil until the end came,
death after his crimes. Then it became clear,
obvious to everyone once the fight was over,
that an avenger lurked and was still alive,
grimly biding time. Grendel's mother,
monstrous hell-bride, brooded on her wrongs.
She had been forced down into fearful waters,
the cold depths, after Cain had killed
his father's son, felled his own
brother with a sword. Branded an outlaw,
marked by having murdered, he moved into the wilds,
shunned company and joy. And from Cain there sprang
misbegotten spirits, among them Grendel,
the banished and accursed, due to come to grips
with that watcher in Heorot waiting to do battle.
The monster wrenched and wrestled with him
but Beowulf was mindful of his mighty strength,
the wondrous gifts God had showered on him:
he relied for help on the Lord of All,
on His care and favour. So he overcame the foe,
brought down the hell-brute. Broken and bowed,
outcast from all sweetness, the enemy of mankind
made for his death-den. But now his mother

had sallied forth on a savage journey,
grief-racked and ravenous, desperate for revenge.

She came to Heorot. There, inside the hall,   Grendel's mother
attacks.
Danes lay asleep, earls who would soon endure
a great reversal, once Grendel's mother
attacked and entered. Her onslaught was less
only by as much as an amazon warrior's
strength is less than an armed man's
when the hefted sword, its hammered edge
and gleaming blade slathered in blood,
razes the sturdy boar-ridge off a helmet.
Then in the hall, hard-honed swords
were grabbed from the bench, many a broad shield
lifted and braced; there was little thought of helmets
or woven mail when they woke in terror.

The hell-dam was in panic, desperate to get out,
in mortal terror the moment she was found.
She had pounced and taken one of the retainers
in a tight hold, then headed for the fen.
To Hrothgar, this man was the most beloved
of the friends he trusted between the two seas.
She had done away with a great warrior,
ambushed him at rest.
                              Beowulf was elsewhere.
Earlier, after the award of the treasure,
the Geat had been given another lodging.

There was uproar in Heorot. She had snatched their trophy,
Grendel's bloodied arm. It was a fresh blow
to the afflicted bawn. The bargain was hard,
both parties having to pay
with the lives of friends. And the old lord,
the grey-haired warrior, was heartsore and weary
when he heard the news: his highest placed adviser,
his dearest companion, was dead and gone.

Beowulf was quickly brought to the chamber:
the winner of fights, the arch-warrior,
came first-footing in with his fellow troops
to where the king in his wisdom waited,
still wondering whether Almighty God
would ever turn the tide of his misfortunes.
So Beowulf entered with his band in attendance
and the wooden floor-boards banged and rang
as he advanced, hurrying to address
the prince of the Ingwins, asking if he'd rested,
since the urgent summons had come as a surprise.

Hrothgar laments
the death of his
counsellor. He
knows Grendel's
mother must
avenge her son.
Then Hrothgar, the Shieldings' helmet, spoke:
'Rest? What is rest? Sorrow has returned.
Alas for the Danes! Aeschere is dead.
He was Yrmenlaf's elder brother
and a soul-mate to me, a true mentor,
my right-hand man when the ranks clashed
and our boar-crests had to take a battering
in the line of action. Aeschere was everything
the world admires in a wise man and a friend.
Then this roaming killer came in a fury
and slaughtered him in Heorot. Where she is hiding,
glutting on the corpse and glorying in her escape,
I cannot tell; she has taken up the feud
because of last night, when you killed Grendel,
wrestled and racked him in ruinous combat
since for too long he had terrorized us
with his depredations. He died in battle,
paid with his life; and now this powerful
other one arrives, this force for evil
driven to avenge her kinsman's death.
Or so it seems to thanes in their grief,
in the anguish every thane endures
at the loss of a ring-giver, now that the hand
that bestowed so richly has been stilled in death.

'I have heard it said by my people in hall,
counsellors who live in the upland country,
that they have seen two such creatures
prowling the moors, huge marauders
from some other world. One of these things,
as far as anyone can ever discern,
looks like a woman; the other, warped
in the shape of a man, moves beyond the pale
bigger than any man, an unnatural birth
called Grendel by the country people
in former days. They are fatherless creatures,
and their whole ancestry is hidden in a past
of demons and ghosts. They dwell apart
among wolves on the hills, on windswept crags
and treacherous keshes, where cold streams
pour down the mountain and disappear
under mist and moorland.

The country
people's tales about
the monsters.

                      A few miles from here
a frost-stiffened wood waits and keeps watch
above a mere; the overhanging bank
is a maze of tree-roots mirrored in its surface.
At night there, something uncanny happens:
the water burns. And the mere-bottom
has never been sounded by the sons of men.
On its bank, the heather-stepper halts:
the hart in flight from pursuing hounds
will turn to face them with firm-set horns
and die in the wood rather than dive
beneath its surface. That is no good place.
When wind blows up and stormy weather
makes clouds scud and the skies weep,
out of its depths a dirty surge
is pitched towards the heavens. Now help depends
again on you and on you alone.
The gap of danger where the demon waits
is still unknown to you. Seek it if you dare.

The haunted mere.

[1345–79]

I will compensate you for settling the feud
as I did the last time with lavish wealth,
coffers of coiled gold, if you come back.'

Beowulf bolsters
Hrothgar's courage.
He proclaims the
heroic code that
guides their lives. Beowulf, son of Ecgtheow, spoke:
'Wise sir, do not grieve. It is always better
to avenge dear ones than to indulge in mourning.
For every one of us, living in this world
means waiting for our end. Let whoever can
win glory before death. When a warrior is gone,
that will be his best and only bulwark.
So arise, my lord, and let us immediately
set forth on the trail of this troll-dam.
I guarantee you: she will not get away,
not to dens under ground nor upland groves
nor the ocean floor. She'll have nowhere to flee to.
Endure your troubles today. Bear up
and be the man I expect you to be.'

The expedition to
the mere. With that the old lord sprang to his feet
and praised God for Beowulf's pledge.
Then a bit and halter were brought for his horse
with the plaited mane. The wise king mounted
the royal saddle and rode out in style
with a force of shield-bearers. The forest paths
were marked all over with the monster's tracks,
her trail on the ground wherever she had gone
across dark moorland, dragging away
the body of that thane, Hrothgar's best
counsellor and overseer of the country.
So the noble prince proceeded undismayed
up fells and screes, along narrow footpaths
and ways where they were forced into single file,
ledges on cliffs above lairs of water-monsters.
He went in front with a few men,
good judges of the lie of the land,

and suddenly discovered the dismal wood,
mountain trees growing out at an angle
above grey stones: the bloodshot water
surged underneath. It was a sore blow
to all of the Danes, friends of the Shieldings,
a hurt to each and every one
of that noble company when they came upon
Aeschere's head at the foot of the cliff.

Everybody gazed as the hot gore
kept wallowing up and an urgent war-horn
repeated its notes: the whole party
sat down to watch. The water was infested
with all kinds of reptiles. There were writhing sea-dragons
and monsters slouching on slopes by the cliff,
serpents and wild things such as those that often
surface at dawn to roam the sail-road
and doom the voyage. Down they plunged,
lashing in anger at the loud call
of the battle-bugle. An arrow from the bow
of the Geat chief got one of them
as he surged to the surface: the seasoned shaft
stuck deep in his flank and his freedom in the water
got less and less. It was his last swim.
He was swiftly overwhelmed in the shallows,
prodded by barbed boar-spears,
cornered, beaten, pulled up on the bank,
a strange lake-birth, a loathsome catch
men gazed at in awe.
                            Beowulf got ready,
donned his war-gear, indifferent to death;
his mighty, hand-forged, fine-webbed mail
would soon meet with the menace under water.
It would keep the bone-cage of his body safe:
no enemy's clasp could crush him in it,
no vicious armlock choke his life out.

Beowulf arms for
the underwater
fight.

To guard his head he had a glittering helmet
that was due to be muddied on the mere-bottom
and blurred in the upswirl. It was of beaten gold,
princely headgear hooped and hasped
by a weapon-smith who had worked wonders
in days gone by and embellished it with boar-shapes;
since then it had resisted every sword.
And another item lent by Unferth
at that moment of need was of no small importance:
the brehon handed him a hilted weapon,
a rare and ancient sword named Hrunting.
The iron blade with its ill-boding patterns
had been tempered in blood. It had never failed
the hand of anyone who hefted it in battle,
anyone who had fought and faced the worst
in the gap of danger. This was not the first time
it had been called to perform heroic feats.

When he lent that blade to the better swordsman,
Unferth, the strong-built son of Ecglaf,
could hardly have remembered the ranting speech
he had made in his cups. He was not man enough
to face the turmoil of a fight under water
and the risk to his life. So there he lost
fame and repute. It was different for the other
rigged out in his gear, ready to do battle.

Beowulf takes his leave.

Beowulf, son of Ecgtheow, spoke:
'Wisest of kings, now that I have come
to the point of action, I ask you to recall
what we said earlier: that you, son of Halfdane
and gold-friend to retainers, that you, if I should fall
and suffer death while serving your cause,
would act like a father to me afterwards.
If this combat kills me, take care
of my young company, my comrades in arms.

And be sure also, my beloved Hrothgar,
to send Hygelac the treasures I received.
Let the lord of the Geats gaze on that gold,
let Hrethel's son take note of it and see
that I found a ring-giver of rare magnificence
and enjoyed the good of his generosity.
And Unferth is to have what I inherited:
to that far-famed man I bequeath my own
sharp-honed, wave-sheened wonderblade.
With Hrunting I shall gain glory or die.'

After these words, the prince of the Weather-Geats
was impatient to be away and plunged suddenly:
without more ado, he dived into the heaving
depths of the lake. It was the best part of a day
before he could see the solid bottom.

Quickly the one who haunted those waters,
who had scavenged and gone her gluttonous rounds
for a hundred seasons, sensed a human
observing her outlandish lair from above.
So she lunged and clutched and managed to catch him
in her brutal grip; but his body, for all that,
remained unscathed: the mesh of the chain-mail
saved him on the outside. Her savage talons
failed to rip the web of his war-shirt.
Then once she touched bottom, that wolfish swimmer
carried the ring-mailed prince to her court
so that for all his courage he could never use
the weapons he carried; and a bewildering horde
came at him from the depths, droves of sea-beasts
who attacked with tusks and tore at his chain-mail
in a ghastly onslaught. The gallant man
could see he had entered some hellish turn-hole
and yet the water did not work against him
because the hall-roofing held off

*Beowulf is captured
by Grendel's
mother.*

the force of the current; then he saw firelight,
a gleam and flare-up, a glimmer of brightness.

The hero observed that swamp-thing from hell,
the tarn-hag in all her terrible strength,
then heaved his war-sword and swung his arm:
the decorated blade came down ringing

His sword fails to do damage.

and singing on her head. But he soon found
his battle-torch extinguished: the shining blade
refused to bite. It spared her and failed
the man in his need. It had gone through many
a hand-to-hand fight, had hewed the armour
and helmets of the doomed, but here at last
the fabulous powers of that heirloom failed.

Hygelac's kinsman kept thinking about
his name and fame: he never lost heart.

He fights back with his bare hands.

Then, in a fury, he flung his sword away.
The keen, inlaid, worm-loop-patterned steel
was hurled to the ground: he would have to rely
on the might of his arm. So must a man do
who intends to gain enduring glory
in a combat. Life doesn't cost him a thought.
Then the prince of War-Geats, warming to this fight
with Grendel's mother, gripped her shoulder
and laid about him in a battle frenzy:
he pitched his killer opponent to the floor
but she rose quickly and retaliated,
grappled him tightly in her grim embrace.
The sure-footed fighter felt suddenly daunted,
the strongest of warriors stumbled and fell.
So she pounced upon him and pulled out
a broad, whetted knife: now she would avenge
her only child. But the mesh of chain-mail
on Beowulf's shoulder shielded his life,
turned the edge and tip of the blade.

[1516–49]

The son of Ecgtheow would surely have perished
and the Geats lost their warrior under the wide earth
had the strong links and locks of his war-gear
not helped to save him: holy God
decided the victory. It was easy for the Lord,
the Ruler of Heaven, to redress the balance
once Beowulf got back on his feet.

Then he saw a blade that boded well,
a sword in her armoury, an ancient heirloom
from the days of the giants, an ideal weapon,
one that any warrior would envy,
but so huge and heavy of itself
only Beowulf could wield it in battle.
So the Shieldings' hero, hard-pressed and enraged,
took a firm hold of the hilt and swung
the blade in an arc, a resolute blow
that bit deep into her neck-bone
and severed it entirely, toppling the doomed
house of her flesh; she fell to the floor.
The sword dripped blood, the swordsman was elated.

Beowulf discovers a
mighty sword and
slays his opponent.

A light appeared and the place brightened
the way the sky does when heaven's candle
is shining clearly. He inspected the vault:
with sword held high, its hilt raised
to guard and threaten, Hygelac's thane
scouted along the wall in Grendel's wake.
Now the weapon was to prove its worth.
The warrior determined to take revenge
for every gross act Grendel had committed –
and not only for that one occasion
when he'd come to slaughter the sleeping troops,
fifteen of Hrothgar's house-guards
surprised on their benches and ruthlessly devoured,
and as many again carried away,

He proceeds to
behead Grendel's
corpse.

[1550–83]

a brutal plunder. Beowulf in his fury
now settled that score: he saw the monster
in his resting-place, war-weary and wrecked,
a lifeless corpse, a casualty
of the battle in Heorot. The body gaped
at the stroke dealt to it after death:
Beowulf cut the corpse's head off.

Forebodings of
those on the shore.
Immediately the counsellors keeping a lookout
with Hrothgar, watching the lake water,
saw a heave-up and surge of waves
and blood in the backwash. They bowed grey heads,
spoke in their sage, experienced way
about the good warrior, how they never again
expected to see that prince returning
in triumph to their king. It was clear to many
that the wolf of the deep had destroyed him forever.

The ninth hour of the day arrived.
The brave Shieldings abandoned the cliff-top
and the king went home; but sick at heart,
staring at the mere, the strangers held on.
They wished, without hope, to behold their lord,
Beowulf himself.

The sword-blade
melts.
                    Meanwhile, the sword
began to wilt into gory icicles,
to slather and thaw. It was a wonderful thing,
the way it all melted as ice melts
when the Father eases the fetters off the frost
and unravels the water-ropes, He who wields power
over time and tide: He is the true Lord.

Beowulf returns
with the sword's
hilt and Grendel's
head.
The Geat captain saw treasure in abundance
but carried no spoils from those quarters
except for the head and the inlaid sword-hilt
embossed with jewels; its blade had melted

and the scrollwork on it burnt, so scalding was the blood
of the poisonous fiend who had perished there.
Then away he swam, the one who had survived
the fall of his enemies, flailing to the surface.
The wide water, the waves and pools,
were no longer infested once the wandering fiend
let go of her life and this unreliable world.
The seafarers' leader made for land,
resolutely swimming, delighted with his prize,
the mighty load he was lugging to the surface.
His thanes advanced in a troop to meet him,
thanking God and taking great delight
in seeing their prince back safe and sound.
Quickly the hero's helmet and mail-shirt
were loosed and unlaced. The lake settled,
clouds darkened above the bloodshot depths.

With high hearts they headed away
along footpaths and trails through the fields,
roads that they knew, each of them wrestling
with the head they were carrying from the lakeside cliff,
men kingly in their courage and capable
of difficult work. It was a task for four
to hoist Grendel's head on a spear
and bear it under strain to the bright hall.
But soon enough they neared the place,
fourteen Geats in fine fettle,
striding across the outlying ground
in a delighted throng around their leader.

In he came then, the thanes' commander,   He displays the
the arch-warrior, to address Hrothgar: head in Heorot.
his courage was proven, his glory was secure.
Grendel's head was hauled by the hair,
dragged across the floor where the people were drinking,
a horror for both queen and company to behold.

They stared in awe. It was an astonishing sight.

A brief account of
the fight.
Beowulf, son of Ecgtheow, spoke:
'So, son of Halfdane, prince of the Shieldings,
we are glad to bring this booty from the lake.
It is a token of triumph and we tender it to you.
I barely survived the battle under water.
It was hard fought, a desperate affair
that could have gone badly; if God had not helped me,
the outcome would have been quick and fatal.
Although Hrunting is hard-edged,
I could never bring it to bear in battle.
But the Lord of Men allowed me to behold
an ancient sword shining on the wall –
for he often helps the unbefriended –
a weapon made for giants, there for the wielding.
Then my moment came in the combat and I struck
the dwellers in that den. Next thing the damascened
swordblade melted; it bloated and it burned
in their rushing blood. I have wrestled the hilt
from the enemies' hand, avenged the evil
done to the Danes; it is what was due.
And this I pledge, O prince of the Shieldings:
you can sleep secure with your company of troops
in Heorot Hall. Never need you fear
for a single thane of your sept or nation,
young warriors or old, that laying waste of life
that you and your people endured of yore.'

Beowulf presents
the sword-hilt to
Hrothgar.
Then the golden hilt was handed over
to the old lord, a relic from long ago
for the venerable ruler. That rare smithwork
was passed on to the prince of the Danes
when those devils perished; once death removed
that murdering, guilt-steeped, God-cursed fiend,
eliminating his unholy life

and his mother's as well, it was willed to that king
who of all the lavish gift-lords of the north
was the best regarded between the two seas.

Hrothgar spoke; he examined the hilt,
that relic of old times. It was engraved all over
and showed how war first came into the world
and flood destroyed the tribe of giants.
They suffered a terrible severance from the Lord;
the Almighty made the waters rise,
drowned them in the deluge for retribution.
In pure gold inlay on the sword-guards
there were rune-markings correctly incised,
stating and recording for whom the sword
had been first made and ornamented
with its scroll-worked hilt. Then everyone hushed
as the son of Halfdane spoke this wisdom:
'A protector of his people, pledged to uphold
truth and justice and to respect tradition,   Hrothgar's address
is entitled to affirm that this man   to Beowulf.
was born to distinction. Beowulf, my friend,
your fame has gone far and wide,
you are known everywhere. In all things you are
    even-tempered,
prudent and resolute. So I stand firm by the promise of
    friendship
we exchanged before. Forever you will be
your people's mainstay and your own warriors'
helping hand.
                Heremod was different,   He contrasts
the way he behaved to Ecgwala's sons.   Beowulf with King
His rise in the world brought little joy   Heremod.
to the Danish people, only death and destruction.
He vented his rage on men he caroused with,
killed his own comrades, a pariah king
who cut himself off from his own kind,

even though Almighty God had made him
eminent and powerful and marked him from the start
for a happy life. But a change happened,
he grew bloodthirsty, gave no more rings
to honour the Danes. He suffered in the end
for having plagued his people for so long:
his life lost happiness.
                            So learn from this
and understand true worth. I who am telling you
have wintered into wisdom.

Hrothgar's
discourse on the
dangers of power.   It is a great wonder
how Almighty God in His magnificence
favours our race with rank and scope
and the gift of wisdom; His sway is wide.
Sometimes He allows the mind of a man
of distinguished birth to follow its bent,
grants him fulfilment and felicity on earth
and forts to command in his own country.
He permits him to lord it in many lands
until the man in his unthinkingness
forgets that it will ever end for him.
He indulges his desires; illness and old age
mean nothing to him; his mind is untroubled
by envy or malice or the thought of enemies
with their hate-honed swords. The whole world
conforms to his will, he is kept from the worst
until an element of overweening
enters into him and takes hold
while the soul's guard, its sentry, drowses,
grown too distracted. A killer stalks him,
an archer who draws a deadly bow.
And then the man is hit in the heart,
the arrow flies beneath his defences,
the devious promptings of the demon start.
His old possessions seem paltry to him now.
He covets and resents; dishonours custom

and bestows no gold; and because of good things
that the Heavenly Powers gave him in the past
he ignores the shape of things to come.
Then finally the end arrives
when the body he was lent collapses and falls
prey to its death; ancestral possessions
and the goods he hoarded are inherited by another
who lets them go with a liberal hand.

'O flower of warriors, beware of that trap.
Choose, dear Beowulf, the better part,
eternal rewards. Do not give way to pride.
For a brief while your strength is in bloom
but it fades quickly; and soon there will follow
illness or the sword to lay you low,
or a sudden fire or surge of water
or jabbing blade or javelin from the air
or repellent age. Your piercing eye
will dim and darken; and death will arrive,
dear warrior, to sweep you away.

Beowulf is exhorted
to be mindful of the
fragility of life.

'Just so I ruled the Ring-Danes' country
for fifty years, defended them in wartime
with spear and sword against constant assaults
by many tribes: I came to believe
my enemies had faded from the face of the earth.
Still, what happened was a hard reversal
from bliss to grief. Grendel struck
after lying in wait. He laid waste to the land
and from that moment my mind was in dread
of his depredations. So I praise God
in His heavenly glory that I lived to behold
this head dripping blood and that after such harrowing
I can look upon it in triumph at last.
Take your place, then, with pride and pleasure
and move to the feast. Tomorrow morning

No life is immune
to danger:
Hrothgar's
experience proves
it.

our treasure will be shared and showered upon you.'

A feast. The
warriors rest.
The Geat was elated and gladly obeyed
the old man's bidding; he sat on the bench.
And soon all was restored, the same as before.
Happiness came back, the hall was thronged,
and a banquet set forth; black night fell
and covered them in darkness.
                Then the company rose
for the old campaigner: the grey-haired prince
was ready for bed. And a need for rest
came over the brave shield-bearing Geat.
He was a weary seafarer, far from home,
so immediately a house-guard guided him out,
one whose office entailed looking after
whatever a thane on the road in those days
might need or require. It was noble courtesy.

That great heart rested. The hall towered,
gold-shingled and gabled, and the guest slept in it
until the black raven with raucous glee
announced heaven's joy, and a hurry of brightness
overran the shadows. Warriors rose quickly,
impatient to be off: their own country
was beckoning the nobles; and the bold voyager
longed to be aboard his distant boat.
Then that stalwart fighter ordered Hrunting
to be brought to Unferth, and bade Unferth
take the sword and thanked him for lending it.
He said he had found it a friend in battle
and a powerful help; he put no blame
on the blade's cutting edge. He was a considerate man.

Beowulf and his
band prepare to
depart.
And there the warriors stood in their war-gear,
eager to go, while their honoured lord
approached the platform where the other sat.

The undaunted hero addressed Hrothgar.
Beowulf, son of Ecgtheow, spoke:
'Now we who crossed the wide sea
have to inform you that we feel a desire
to return to Hygelac. Here we have been welcomed
and thoroughly entertained. You have treated us well.
If there is any favour on earth I can perform
beyond deeds of arms I have done already,
anything that would merit your affections more,
I shall act, my lord, with alacrity.
If ever I hear from across the ocean
that people on your borders are threatening battle
as attackers have done from time to time,
I shall land with a thousand thanes at my back
to help your cause. Hygelac may be young
to rule a nation, but this much I know
about the king of the Geats: he will come to my aid
and want to support me by word and action
in your hour of need, when honour dictates
that I raise a hedge of spears around you.
Then if Hrethric should think about travelling
as a king's son to the court of the Geats,
he will find many friends. Foreign places
yield more to one who is himself worth meeting.'

Hrothgar spoke and answered him:
'The Lord in his wisdom sent you those words
and they came from the heart. I have never heard
so young a man make truer observations.
You are strong in body and mature in mind,
impressive in speech. If it should come to pass
that Hrethel's descendant dies beneath a spear,
if deadly battle or the sword-blade or disease
fells the prince who guards your people
and you are still alive, then I firmly believe
the seafaring Geats won't find a man

Hrothgar declares
that Beowulf is fit
to be king of the
Geats.

worthier of acclaim as their king and defender
than you, if only you would undertake
the lordship of your homeland. My liking for you
deepens with time, dear Beowulf.
What you have done is to draw two peoples,
the Geat nation and us neighbouring Danes,
into shared peace and a pact of friendship
in spite of hatreds we have harboured in the past.
For as long as I rule this far-flung land
treasures will change hands and each side will treat
the other with gifts; across the gannet's bath,
over the broad sea, whorled prows will bring
presents and tokens. I know your people
are beyond reproach in every respect,
steadfast in the old way with friend or foe.'

Gifts presented,
farewells taken.

Then the earls' defender furnished the hero
with twelve treasures and told him to set out,
sail home safely with those gifts
to the people he loved, but to return promptly.
And so the good and grey-haired Dane,
that high-born king, kissed Beowulf
and embraced his neck, then broke down
in sudden tears. Two forebodings
disturbed him in his wisdom, but one was stronger:
nevermore would they meet each other
face to face. And such was his affection
that he could not help being overcome:
his fondness for the man was so deep-founded,
it warmed his heart and wound the heartstrings
tight in his breast.
                    The embrace ended
and Beowulf, glorious in his gold regalia,
stepped the green earth. Straining at anchor
and ready for boarding, his boat awaited him.
So they went on their journey, and Hrothgar's generosity

[1851–84]

was praised repeatedly. He was a peerless king
until old age sapped his strength and did him
mortal harm, as it has done so many.

Down to the waves then, dressed in the web
of their chain-mail and war-shirts, the young men marched
in high spirits. The coast-guard spied them,
thanes setting forth, the same as before.
His salute this time from the top of the cliff
was far from unmannerly; he galloped to meet them
and as they took ship in their shining gear,
he said how welcome they would be in Geatland.
Then the broad hull was beached on the sand
to be cargoed with treasure, horses and war-gear.
The curved prow motioned; the mast stood high
above Hrothgar's riches in the loaded hold.

The guard who had watched the boat was given
a sword with gold fittings and in future days
that present would make him a respected man
at his place on the mead-bench.
                            Then the keel plunged
and shook in the sea; and they sailed from Denmark.

Right away the mast was rigged with its sea-shawl;
sail-ropes were tightened, timbers drummed
and stiff winds kept the wave-crosser
skimming ahead; as she heaved forward,
her foamy neck was fleet and buoyant,
a lapped prow loping over currents,
until finally the Geats caught sight of coastline
and familiar cliffs. The keel reared up,
wind lifted it home, it hit on the land.

The harbour guard came hurrying out
to the rolling water: he had watched the offing

The Geats march
back to the shore.

They sail from
Denmark.

They arrive at
Hygelac's stronghold.

long and hard, on the lookout for those friends.
With the anchor cables, he moored their craft
right where it had beached, in case a backwash
might catch the hull and carry it away.
Then he ordered the prince's treasure-trove
to be carried ashore. It was a short step
from there to where Hrethel's son and heir,
Hygelac the gold-giver, makes his home
on a secure cliff, in the company of retainers.

Queen Hygd
introduced. The
story of Queen
Modthryth,
Hygd's opposite, is
told by the poet. The building was magnificent, the king majestic,
ensconced in his hall; and although Hygd, his queen,
was young, a few short years at court,
her mind was thoughtful and her manners sure.
Haereth's daughter behaved generously
and stinted nothing when she distributed
bounty to the Geats.
                          Great Queen Modthryth
perpetrated terrible wrongs.
If any retainer ever made bold
to look her in the face, if an eye not her lord's
stared at her directly during daylight,
the outcome was sealed: he was kept bound
in hand-tightened shackles, racked, tortured
until doom was pronounced – death by the sword,
slash of blade, blood-gush and death-qualms
in an evil display. Even a queen
outstanding in beauty must not overstep like that.
A queen should weave peace, not punish the innocent
with loss of life for imagined insults.
But Hemming's kinsman put a halt to her ways
and drinkers round the table had another tale:
she was less of a bane to people's lives,
less cruel-minded, after she was married
to the brave Offa, a bride arrayed
in her gold finery, given away

62

by a caring father, ferried to her young prince
over dim seas. In days to come
she would grace the throne and grow famous
for her good deeds and conduct of life,
her high devotion to the hero king
who was the best king, it has been said,
between the two seas or anywhere else
on the face of the earth. Offa was honoured
far and wide for his generous ways,
his fighting spirit and his far-seeing
defence of his homeland; from him there sprang Eomer,
Garmund's grandson, kinsman of Hemming,
his warriors' mainstay and master of the field.

Heroic Beowulf and his band of men   Beowulf and his
crossed the wide strand, striding along   troop are welcomed
the sandy foreshore; the sun shone,   in Hygelac's hall.
the world's candle warmed them from the south
as they hastened to where, as they had heard,
the young king, Ongentheow's killer
and his people's protector, was dispensing rings
inside his bawn. Beowulf's return
was reported to Hygelac as soon as possible,
news that the captain was now in the enclosure,
his battle-brother back from the fray
alive and well, walking to the hall.
Room was quickly made, on the king's orders,
and the troops filed across the cleared floor.

After Hygelac had offered greetings
to his loyal thane in lofty speech,
he and his kinsman, that hale survivor,
sat face to face. Haereth's daughter
moved about with the mead-jug in her hand,
taking care of the company, filling the cups
that warriors held out. Then Hygelac began

to put courteous questions to his old comrade
in the high hall. He hankered to know
every tale the Sea-Geats had to tell.

Hygelac questions
Beowulf.
'How did you fare on your foreign voyage,
dear Beowulf, when you abruptly decided
to sail away across the salt water
and fight at Heorot? Did you help Hrothgar
much in the end? Could you ease the prince
of his well-known troubles? Your undertaking
cast my spirits down, I dreaded the outcome
of your expedition and pleaded with you
long and hard to leave the killer be,
let the South-Danes settle their own
blood-feud with Grendel. So God be thanked
I am granted this sight of you, safe and sound.'

Beowulf tells what
happened in the
land of the Danes.
Beowulf, son of Ecgtheow, spoke:
'What happened, Lord Hygelac, is hardly a secret
any more among men in this world –
myself and Grendel coming to grips
on the very spot where he visited destruction
on the Victory-Shieldings and violated
life and limb, losses I avenged
so no earthly offspring of Grendel's
need ever boast of that bout before dawn,
no matter how long the last of his evil
family survives.
                  When I first landed
I proceeded to the ring-hall and saluted Hrothgar.
Once he discovered why I had come
the son of Halfdane sent me immediately
to sit with his own sons on the bench.
It was a happy gathering. In my whole life
I have never seen mead enjoyed more
in any hall on earth. Sometimes the queen

herself appeared, peace-pledge between nations,
to hearten the young ones and hand out
a torque to a warrior, then take her place.
Sometimes Hrothgar's daughter distributed
ale to older ranks, in order on the benches:
I heard the company call her Freawaru
as she made her rounds, presenting men
with the gem-studded bowl, young bride-to-be
to the gracious Ingeld, in her gold-trimmed attire.
The friend of the Shieldings favours her betrothal:
the guardian of the kingdom sees good in it
and hopes this woman will heal old wounds
and grievous feuds.

He foresees the
grim consequence
of a proposed
marriage.

                        But generally the spear
is prompt to retaliate when a prince is killed,
no matter how admirable the bride may be.

'Think how the Heathobards will be bound to feel,
their lord, Ingeld, and his loyal thanes,
when he walks in with that woman to the feast:
Danes are at the table, being entertained,
honoured guests in glittering regalia,
burnished ring-mail that was their hosts' birthright,
looted when the Heathobards could no longer wield
their weapons in the shield-clash, when they went down
with their beloved comrades and forfeited their lives.
Then an old spearman will speak while they are drinking,
having glimpsed some heirloom that brings alive
memories of the massacre; his mood will darken
and heart-stricken, in the stress of his emotion,
he will begin to test a young man's temper
and stir up trouble, starting like this:
"Now, my friend, don't you recognize
your father's sword, his favourite weapon,
the one he wore when he went out in his war-mask
to face the Danes on that final day.

When the Danes
appear at
Freawaru's
wedding, their
hosts, the
Heathobards, will
be stirred to avenge
an old defeat.

After Wethergeld died and his men were doomed
the Shieldings quickly claimed the field,
and now here's a son of one or other
of those same killers coming through our hall
overbearing us, mouthing boasts,
and rigged in armour that by right is yours."
And so he keeps on, recalling and accusing,
working things up with bitter words
until one of the lady's retainers lies
spattered in blood, split open
on his father's account. The killer knows
the lie of the land and escapes with his life.
Then on both sides the oath-bound lords
will break the peace, a passionate hate
will build up in Ingeld and love for his bride
will falter in him as the feud rankles.
I therefore suspect the good faith of the Heathobards,
the truth of their friendship and the trustworthiness
of their alliance with the Danes.

The tale of the fight with Grendel resumes.   But now, my lord,
I shall carry on with my account of Grendel,
the whole story of everything that happened
in the hand-to-hand fight.

                                    After heaven's gem
had gone mildly to earth, that maddened spirit,
the terror of those twilights, came to attack us
where we stood guard, still safe inside the hall.
There deadly violence came down on Handscio
and he fell as fate ordained, the first to perish,
rigged out for the combat. A comrade from our ranks
had come to grief in Grendel's maw:
he ate up the entire body.
There was blood on his teeth, he was bloated and dangerous,
all roused up, yet still unready
to leave the hall empty-handed;
renowned for his might, he matched himself against me,

66   [2051–84]

wildly reaching. He had this roomy pouch,
a strange accoutrement, intricately strung
and hung at the ready, a rare patchwork
of devilishly fitted dragon-skins.
I had done him no wrong, yet the raging demon
wanted to cram me and many another
into this bag – but it was not to be
once I got to my feet in a blind fury.
It would take too long to tell how I repaid
the terror of the land for every life he took
and so won credit for you, my king,
and for all your people. And although he got away
to enjoy life's sweetness for a while longer,
his right hand stayed behind him in Heorot,
evidence of his miserable overthrow
as he dived into murk on the mere-bottom.

'I got lavish rewards from the lord of the Danes
for my part in the battle, beaten gold
and much else, once morning came
and we took our places at the banquet table.
There was singing and excitement: an old reciter,
a carrier of stories, recalled the early days.
At times some hero made the timbered harp
tremble with sweetness, or related true
and tragic happenings; at times the king
gave the proper turn to some fantastic tale,
or a battle-scarred veteran, bowed with age,
would begin to remember the martial deeds
of his youth and prime and be overcome
as the past welled up in his wintry heart.

'We were happy there the whole day long
and enjoyed our time until another night
descended upon us. Then, with sudden despatch,
the vehement mother avenged her son

Beowulf recalls the
feast in Heorot.

He tells about
Grendel's mother.

and wrought destruction. Death had robbed her,
Geats had slain Grendel, so his ghastly dam
struck back and with bare-faced defiance
laid a man low. Thus life departed
from the sage Aeschere, an elder wise in counsel.
But afterwards, on the morning following,
the Danes could not burn the dead body
nor lay the remains of the man they loved
on his funeral pyre. She had fled with the corpse
and taken refuge beneath torrents on the mountain.
It was a hard blow for Hrothgar to bear,
harder than any he had undergone before.
And so the heartsore king besought me
in your royal name to take my chances
under water, to win glory
and prove my worth. He promised me rewards.
Hence, as is well known, I went to my encounter
with the terror-monger at the bottom of the tarn.
For a while it was hand-to-hand between us,
then blood went curling along the currents
and I beheaded Grendel's mother in the hall
with a mighty sword. I barely managed
to escape with my life; my time had not yet come.
But Halfdane's heir, the shelter of those earls,
again endowed me with a multitude of gifts.

'Thus the king acted with due custom.
I was paid and recompensed completely,
given full measure and the freedom to choose
from Hrothgar's treasures by Hrothgar himself.
These, King Hygelac, I am happy to present
to you as gifts. It is still upon your grace
that all favour depends. I have few kinsmen
who are close, my king, except for your kind self.'

Beowulf presents   Then he ordered the boar-framed standard to be brought,

the battle-topping helmet, the mail-shirt grey as hoar-frost
and the precious war-sword; and proceeded with his speech.

Hygelac with the treasures he has won.

'When Hrothgar presented this war-gear to me
he instructed me, my lord, to give you some account
of why it signifies his special favour.
He said it had belonged to his older brother,
King Heorogar, who had long kept it,
but that Heorogar had never bequeathed it
to his son Heoroweard, that worthy scion,
loyal as he was. Enjoy it well.'

I heard four horses were handed over next.
Beowulf bestowed four bay steeds
to go with the armour, swift gallopers,
all alike. So ought a kinsman act,
instead of plotting and planning in secret
to bring people to grief, or conspiring to arrange
the death of comrades. The warrior king
was uncle to Beowulf and honoured by his nephew:
each was concerned for the other's good.

I heard he presented Hygd with a gorget,
the priceless torque that the prince's daughter,
Wealhtheow, had given him; and three horses,
supple creatures, brilliantly saddled.
The bright necklace would be luminous on Hygd's breast.

Thus Beowulf bore himself with valour;
he was formidable in battle yet behaved with honour
and took no advantage; never cut down
a comrade who was drunk, kept his temper
and, warrior that he was, watched and controlled
his God-sent strength and his outstanding
natural powers. He had been poorly regarded
for a long time, was taken by the Geats
for less than he was worth: and their lord too

Beowulf's exemplary life is extolled.

[2153–85]   69

had never much esteemed him in the mead-hall.
They firmly believed that he lacked force,
that the prince was a weakling; but presently
every affront to his deserving was reversed.

Hygelac presents
Beowulf with a
sword and great
tracts of land.
The battle-famed king, bulwark of his earls,
ordered a gold-chased heirloom of Hrethel's
to be brought in; it was the best example
of a gem-studded sword in the Geat treasury.
This he laid on Beowulf's lap
and then rewarded him with land as well,
seven thousand hides; and a hall and a throne.
Both owned land by birth in that country,
ancestral grounds; but the greater right
and sway were inherited by the higher born.

Time passes.
Beowulf rules the
Geats for
fifty years.
A lot was to happen in later days
in the fury of battle. Hygelac fell
and the shelter of Heardred's shield proved useless
against the fierce aggression of the Shylfings:
ruthless swordsmen, seasoned campaigners,
they came against him and his conquering nation,
and with cruel force cut him down
so that afterwards
                        the wide kingdom
reverted to Beowulf. He ruled it well
for fifty winters, grew old and wise
as warden of the land

A dragon awakes.
An accidental
theft provokes his
wrath.
                        until one began
to dominate the dark, a dragon on the prowl
from the steep vaults of a stone-roofed barrow
where he guarded a hoard; there was a hidden passage,
unknown to men, but someone managed
to enter by it and interfere
with the heathen trove. He had handled and removed
a gem-studded goblet; it gained him nothing,

though with a thief's wiles he had outwitted
the sleeping dragon and driven him to a fury,
as the people of that country would soon discover.

The intruder who broached the dragon's treasure
and moved him to wrath had never meant to.
It was desperation on the part of a slave
fleeing the heavy hand of some master,
guilt-ridden and on the run,
going to ground. But he soon began
to shake with terror; . . . . . in shock
the wretch . . . .
. . . . panicked and ran
away with the precious . . . . .
metalwork. There were many other
heirlooms heaped inside the earth-house,
because long ago, with deliberate care,
some forgotten person had deposited the whole
rich inheritance of a high-born race
in this ancient cache. Death had come
and taken them all in times gone by
and the one surviving witness of their fate,
the last veteran, could envisage only
the same fate for himself: he foresaw that his joy
in the treasure would be brief.
                              A newly constructed
barrow stood waiting, on a wide headland
close to the waves, its entryway secured.
Into it the keeper of the hoard had carried
all the goods and golden ware
worth preserving. His words were few:
'Now, earth, hold what earls once held
and heroes can no more; it was mined from you first
by honourable men. My own people
have been ruined in war; one by one
they went down to death, looked their last

Long ago, a hoard was hidden in the earth-house by the last survivor of a forgotten race.

on sweet life in the hall. I am left with nobody
to bear a sword or burnish plated goblets,
put a sheen on the cup. The companies have departed.
The hard helmet, hasped with gold,
will be strippéd of its hoops; and the helmet-shiner
who should polish the metal of the war-mask sleeps;
the coat of mail that came through all fights,
through shield-collapse and cut of sword,
decays with the warrior. Nor may webbed mail
range far and wide on the warlord's back
beside his mustered troops. No trembling harp,
no tuned timber, no tumbling hawk
swerving through the hall, no swift horse
pawing the courtyard. Pillage and slaughter
have emptied the earth of entire peoples.'
And so he mourned as he moved about the world,
deserted and alone, lamenting his unhappiness
day and night, until death's flood
brimmed up in his heart.

The dragon nests in   Then an old harrower of the dark
the barrow and   happened to find the hoard open,
guards the gold.   the burning one who hunts out barrows,
the slick-skinned dragon, threatening the night sky
with streamers of fire. People on the farms
are in dread of him. He is driven to hunt out
hoards underground, to guard heathen gold
through age-long vigils, though to little avail.
For three centuries, this scourge of the people
had stood guard on that stoutly protected
underground treasury, until the intruder
unleashed its fury; he hurried to his lord
with the gold-plated cup and made his plea
to be reinstated. Then the vault was rifled,
the ring-hoard robbed, and the wretched man
had his request granted. His master gazed
on that find from the past for the first time.

72   [2252–86]

When the dragon awoke, trouble flared again.
He rippled down the rock, writhing with anger
when he saw the footprints of the prowler who had stolen
too close to his dreaming head.
So may a man not marked by fate
easily escape exile and woe
by the grace of God.   The hoard-guardian
scorched the ground as he scoured and hunted
for the trespasser who had troubled his sleep.
Hot and savage, he kept circling and circling
the outside of the mound. No man appeared
in that desert waste, but he worked himself up
by imagining battle; then back in he'd go
in search of the cup, only to discover
signs that someone had stumbled upon
the golden treasures. So the guardian of the mound,
the hoard-watcher, waited for the gloaming
with fierce impatience; his pent-up fury
at the loss of the vessel made him long to hit back
and lash out in flames. Then, to his delight,
the day waned and he could wait no longer
behind the wall, but hurtled forth
in a fiery blaze. The first to suffer
were the people on the land, but before long
it was their treasure-giver who would come to grief.

The dragon in
turmoil.

The dragon began to belch out flames
and burn bright homesteads; there was a hot glow
that scared everyone, for the vile sky-winger
would leave nothing alive in his wake.
Everywhere the havoc he wrought was in evidence.
Far and near, the Geat nation
bore the brunt of his brutal assaults
and virulent hate. Then back to the hoard
he would dart before daybreak, to hide in his den.

The dragon wreaks
havoc on the Geats.

He had swinged the land, swathed it in flame,
in fire and burning, and now he felt secure
in the vaults of his barrow; but his trust was unavailing.

Beowulf's ominous
feelings about the
dragon. Then Beowulf was given bad news,
a hard truth: his own home,
the best of buildings, had been burnt to a cinder,
the throne-room of the Geats. It threw the hero
into deep anguish and darkened his mood:
the wise man thought he must have thwarted
ancient ordinance of the eternal Lord,
broken His commandment. His mind was in turmoil,
unaccustomed anxiety and gloom
confused his brain; the fire-dragon
had rased the coastal region and reduced
forts and earthworks to dust and ashes,
so the war-king planned and plotted his revenge.
The warrior's protector, prince of the hall-troop,
ordered a marvellous all-iron shield
from his smithy works. He well knew
that linden boards would let him down
and timber burn. After many trials,
he was destined to face the end of his days
in this mortal world; as was the dragon,
for all his long leasehold on the treasure.

Beowulf's pride
and prowess
sustain him. Yet the prince of the rings was too proud
to line up with a large army
against the sky-plague. He had scant regard
for the dragon as a threat, no dread at all
of its courage or strength, for he had kept going
at dangerous times and in tight corners
often in the past, after he had purged
Hrothgar's hall, triumphed in Heorot
in the fight with Grendel. He outgrappled the monster
and his evil kin.

One of his cruellest
hand-to-hand encounters had happened
when Hygelac, king of the Geats, was killed
in Friesland: the people's friend and lord,
Hrethel's son, slaked a swordblade's
thirst for blood. But Beowulf's prodigious
gifts as a swimmer guaranteed his safety:
he arrived at the shore, shouldering thirty
battle-dresses, the booty he had won.
There was little for the Hetware to be happy about
as they shielded their faces and fighting on the ground
began in earnest. With Beowulf against them,
few could hope to return home.

Across the wide sea, desolate and alone,
the son of Ecgtheow swam back to his people.
There Hygd offered him throne and authority
as lord of the ring-hoard: with Hygelac dead,
she had no belief in her son's ability
to defend their homeland against foreign invaders.
Yet there was no way the weakened nation
could get Beowulf to give in and agree
to be elevated over Heardred as his lord
or to undertake the office of kingship.
But he did provide support for the prince,
honoured and minded him until he matured
as the ruler of Geatland.
                    Then over sea-roads
exiles arrived, sons of Ohthere.
They had rebelled against the best of all
the sea-kings in Sweden, the one who held sway
in the Shylfing nation, their renowned prince,
lord of the mead-hall. That marked the end
for Hygelac's son: his hospitality
was mortally rewarded with wounds from a sword.
Heardred lay slaughtered and Onela returned

A flashback:
Hygelac's death,
Beowulf's rearguard
action and escape
across the sea.

Beowulf acts as
counsellor to
Hygelac's heir,
Heardred.

Heardred is
implicated in
Swedish feuds and
slain.

to the land of Sweden, leaving Beowulf
to ascend the throne, to sit in majesty
and rule over the Geats. He was a good king.

*Beowulf inherits
the kingship, settles
the feuding.*
In days to come, he contrived to avenge
the fall of his prince; he befriended Eadgils
when Eadgils was friendless, aiding his cause
with weapons and warriors over the wide sea,
sending him men. The feud was settled
on a comfortless campaign when he killed Onela.

And so the son of Ecgtheow had survived
every extreme, excelling himself
in daring and in danger, until the day arrived
when he had to come face to face with the dragon.

*The day of
reckoning:
Beowulf and his
troop reconnoitre.*
The lord of the Geats took eleven comrades
and went in a rage to reconnoitre.
By then he had discovered the cause of the affliction
being visited on the people. The precious cup
had come to him from the hand of the finder,
the one who had started all this strife
and was now added as a thirteenth to their number.
They press-ganged and compelled this poor creature
to be their guide. Against his will
he led them to the earth-vault he alone knew,
an underground barrow near the billowing sea
and the heave of the waves, heaped inside
with exquisite metalwork. The one who stood guard
was dangerous and watchful, warden of that trove
buried under earth: no easy bargain
would be made in that place by any man.

*Beowulf's
forebodings.*
The veteran king sat down on the cliff-top.
He wished good luck to the Geats who had shared
his hearth and his gold. He was sad at heart,
unsettled yet ready, sensing his death.

[2388–420]

His fate hovered near, unknowable but certain:
it would soon claim his coffered soul,
part life from limb. Before long
the prince's spirit would spin free from his body.

Beowulf, son of Ecgtheow, spoke:
'Many a skirmish I survived when I was young
and many times of war: I remember them well.
At seven, I was fostered out by my father,
left in the charge of my people's lord.
King Hrethel kept me and took care of me,
was open-handed, behaved like a kinsman.
While I was his ward, he treated me no worse
as a wean about the place than one of his own boys,
Herebeald and Haethcyn, or my own Hygelac.
For the eldest, Herebeald, an unexpected
deathbed was laid out, through a brother's doing,
when Haethcyn bent his horn-tipped bow
and loosed the arrow that destroyed his life.
He shot wide and buried a shaft
in the flesh and blood of his own brother.
That offence was beyond redress, a wrongfooting
of the heart's affections; for who could avenge
the prince's life or pay his death-price?
It was like the misery endured by an old man
who has lived to see his son's body
swing on the gallows. He begins to keen
and weep for his boy, watching the raven
gloat where he hangs: he can be of no help.
The wisdom of age is worthless to him.
Morning after morning, he wakes to remember
that his child is gone; he has no interest
in living on until another heir
is born in the hall, now that his first-born
has entered death's dominion for ever.
He gazes sorrowfully at his son's dwelling,

He recalls his early
days as a ward at
King Hrethel's
court.

An accidental
killing and its sad
consequences for
Hrethel.

Hrethel's loss
reflected in 'the
father's lament'.

the banquet hall bereft of all delight,
the windswept hearthstone; the horsemen are sleeping,
the warriors under ground; what was is no more.
No tunes from the harp, no cheer raised in the yard.
Alone with his longing, he lies down on his bed
and sings a lament; everything seems too large,
the steadings and the fields.

                    Such was the feeling
of loss endured by the lord of the Geats
after Herebeald's death. He was helplessly placed
to set to rights the wrong of the murder,
could not punish the killer in accordance with the law
of the blood-feud, although he felt no love for him.
Heartsore, wearied, he turned away
from life's joys, chose God's light
and departed, leaving buildings and lands
to his sons, as a man of substance will.

Beowulf continues
his account of
wars between the
Geats and the
Swedes.
'Then over the wide sea Swedes and Geats
battled and feuded and fought without quarter.
Hostilities broke out when Hrethel died.
Ongentheow's sons were unrelenting,
refusing to make peace, campaigning violently
from coast to coast, constantly setting up
terrible ambushes around Hreosnabeorh.
My own kith and kin avenged
these evil events, as everybody knows,
but the price was high: one of them paid
with his life. Haethcyn, lord of the Geats,
met his fate there and fell in the battle.
The Swedish king,
Ongentheow, dies
at the hands of
Eofor, one of
Hygelac's thanes.
Then, as I have heard, Hygelac's sword
was raised in the morning against Ongentheow,
his brother's killer. When Eofor cleft
the old Swede's helmet, halved it open,
he fell, death-pale: his feud-calloused hand
could not stave off the fatal stroke.

                                                [2456–89]

'The treasures that Hygelac lavished on me
I paid for when I fought, as fortune allowed me,
with my glittering sword. He gave me land
and the security land brings, so he had no call
to go looking for some lesser champion,
some mercenary from among the Gifthas
or the Spear-Danes or the men of Sweden.
I marched ahead of him, always there
at the front of the line; and I shall fight like that
for as long as I live, as long as this sword
shall last, which has stood me in good stead
late and soon, ever since I killed
Dayraven the Frank in front of the two armies.
He brought back no looted breastplate
to the Frisian king, but fell in battle,
their standard-bearer, high-born and brave.
No sword-blade sent him to his death,
my bare hands stilled his heartbeats
and wrecked the bone-house. Now blade and hand,
sword and sword-stroke, will assay the hoard.'

Beowulf recalls his proud days in Hygelac's retinue.

Beowulf spoke, made a formal boast
for the last time: 'I risked my life
often when I was young. Now I am old,
but as king of the people I shall pursue this fight
for the glory of winning, if the evil one will only
abandon his earth-fort and face me in the open.'

Beowulf's last boast.

Then he addressed each dear companion
one final time, those fighters in their helmets,
resolute and high-born: 'I would rather not
use a weapon if I knew another way
to grapple with the dragon and make good my boast
as I did against Grendel in days gone by.
But I shall be meeting molten venom

in the fire he breathes, so I go forth
in mail-shirt and shield. I won't shift a foot
when I meet the cave-guard: what occurs on the wall
between the two of us will turn out as fate,
overseer of men, decides. I am resolved.
I scorn further words against this sky-borne foe.

'Men at arms, remain here on the barrow,
safe in your armour, to see which one of us
is better in the end at bearing wounds
in a deadly fray. This fight is not yours,
nor is it up to any man except me
to measure his strength against the monster
or to prove his worth. I shall win the gold
by my courage, or else mortal combat,
doom of battle, will bear your lord away.'

Then he drew himself up beside his shield.
The fabled warrior in his war-shirt and helmet
trusted in his own strength entirely
and went under the crag. No coward path.

Beowulf fights the dragon. Hard by the rock-face that hale veteran,
a good man who had gone repeatedly
into combat and danger and come through,
saw a stone arch and a gushing stream
that burst from the barrow, blazing and wafting
a deadly heat. It would be hard to survive
unscathed near the hoard, to hold firm
against the dragon in those flaming depths.
Then he gave a shout. The lord of the Geats
unburdened his breast and broke out
in a storm of anger. Under the grey stone
his voice challenged and resounded clearly.
Hate was ignited. The hoard-guard recognized
a human voice, the time was over

for peace and parleying. Pouring forth
in a hot battle-fume, the breath of the monster
burst from the rock. There was a rumble underground.
Down there in the barrow, Beowulf the warrior
lifted his shield: the outlandish thing
writhed and convulsed and viciously
turned on the king, whose keen-edged sword,
an heirloom inherited by ancient right,
was already in his hand. Roused to a fury,
each antagonist struck terror in the other.
Unyielding, the lord of his people loomed
by his tall shield, sure of his ground,
while the serpent looped and unleashed itself.
Swaddled in flames, it came gliding and flexing
and racing towards its fate. Yet his shield defended
the renowned leader's life and limb
for a shorter time than he meant it to:
that final day was the first time
when Beowulf fought and fate denied him
glory in battle. So the king of the Geats
raised his hand and struck hard
at the enamelled scales, but scarcely cut through:
the blade flashed and slashed yet the blow
was far less powerful than the hard-pressed king
had need of at that moment. The mound-keeper
went into a spasm and spouted deadly flames:
when he felt the stroke, battle-fire
billowed and spewed. Beowulf was foiled
of a glorious victory. The glittering sword,
infallible before that day,
failed when he unsheathed it, as it never should have.
For the son of Ecgtheow, it was no easy thing
to have to give ground like that and go
unwillingly to inhabit another home
in a place beyond; so every man must yield
the leasehold of his days.

Beowulf's sword
fails him.

Before long
the fierce contenders clashed again.
The hoard-guard took heart, inhaled and swelled up
and got a new wind; he who had once ruled
was furled in fire and had to face the worst.

All but one of Beowulf's band withdraw to safety.

No help or backing was to be had then
from his high-born comrades; that hand-picked troop
broke ranks and ran for their lives
to the safety of the wood. But within one heart
sorrow welled up: in a man of worth
the claims of kinship cannot be denied.

Wiglaf stands by his lord.

His name was Wiglaf, a son of Weohstan's,
a well-regarded Shylfing warrior
related to Aelfhere. When he saw his lord
tormented by the heat of his scalding helmet,
he remembered the bountiful gifts bestowed on him,
how well he lived among the Waegmundings,
the freehold he inherited from his father before him.
He could not hold back: one hand brandished
the yellow-timbered shield, the other drew his sword –
an ancient blade that was said to have belonged
to Eanmund, the son of Ohthere, the one

The deeds of Wiglaf's father, Weohstan, recalled.

Weohstan had slain when he was an exile without friends.
He carried the arms to the victim's kinfolk,
the burnished helmet, the webbed chain-mail
and that relic of the giants. But Onela returned
the weapons to him, rewarded Weohstan
with Eanmund's war-gear. He ignored the blood-feud,
the fact that Eanmund was his brother's son.

Weohstan kept that war-gear for a lifetime,
the sword and the mail-shirt, until it was the son's turn
to follow his father and perform his part.
Then, in old age, at the end of his days

82

among the Weather-Geats, he bequeathed to Wiglaf
innumerable weapons.
                              And now the youth
was to enter the line of battle with his lord,
his first time to be tested as a fighter.
His spirit did not break and the ancestral blade
would keep its edge, as the dragon discovered
as soon as they came together in the combat.

Sad at heart, addressing his companions,
Wiglaf spoke wise and fluent words:
'I remember that time when mead was flowing,
how we pledged loyalty to our lord in the hall,
promised our ring-giver we would be worth our price,
make good the gift of the war-gear,
those swords and helmets, as and when
his need required it. He picked us out
from the army deliberately, honoured us and judged us
fit for this action, made me these lavish gifts –
and all because he considered us the best
of his arms-bearing thanes. And now, although
he wanted this challenge to be one he'd face
by himself alone – the shepherd of our land,
a man unequalled in the quest for glory
and a name for daring – the day has come
when this lord we serve needs sound men
to give him their support. Let us go to him,
help our leader through the hot flame
and dread of the fire. As God is my witness,
I would rather my body were robed in the same
burning blaze as my gold-giver's body
than go back home bearing arms.
That is unthinkable, unless we have first
slain the foe and defended the life
of the prince of the Weather-Geats. I well know
the things he has done for us deserve better.

Wiglaf's speech to the shirkers.

Why should he alone be left exposed
to fall in battle? We must bond together,
shield and helmet, mail-shirt and sword.'

Wiglaf goes to
Beowulf's aid. Then he waded the dangerous reek and went
under arms to his lord, saying only:
'Go on, dear Beowulf, do everything
you said you would when you were still young
and vowed you would never let your name and fame
be dimmed while you lived. Your deeds are famous,
so stay resolute, my lord, defend your life now
with the whole of your strength. I shall stand by you.'

The dragon attacks
again. After those words, a wildness rose
in the dragon again and drove it to attack,
heaving up fire, hunting for enemies,
the humans it loathed. Flames lapped the shield,
charred it to the boss, and the body-armour
on the young warrior was useless to him.
But Wiglaf did well under the wide rim
Beowulf shared with him once his own had shattered
in sparks and ashes.
                              Inspired again
by the thought of glory, the war-king threw
his whole strength behind a sword-stroke
Another setback. and connected with the skull. And Naegling snapped.
Beowulf's ancient iron-grey sword
let him down in the fight. It was never his fortune
to be helped in combat by the cutting edge
of weapons made of iron. When he wielded a sword,
no matter how blooded and hard-edged the blade,
his hand was too strong, the stroke he dealt
(I have heard) would ruin it. He could reap no advantage.

The dragon's third
onslaught. He
draws blood. Then the bane of that people, the fire-breathing dragon,
was mad to attack for a third time.
When a chance came, he caught the hero

84   [2658–90]

in a rush of flame and clamped sharp fangs
into his neck. Beowulf's body
ran wet with his life-blood: it came welling out.

Next thing, they say, the noble son of Weohstan
saw the king in danger at his side

Wiglaf gets past the
flames and strikes.

and displayed his inborn bravery and strength.
He left the head alone, but his fighting hand
was burned when he came to his kinsman's aid.
He lunged at the enemy lower down
so that his decorated sword sank into its belly
and the flames grew weaker.
                    Once more the king
gathered his strength and drew a stabbing knife

Beowulf delivers the
fatal wound.

he carried on his belt, sharpened for battle.
He stuck it deep into the dragon's flank.
Beowulf dealt it a deadly wound.
They had killed the enemy, courage quelled his life;
that pair of kinsmen, partners in nobility,
had destroyed the foe. So every man should act,
be at hand when needed; but now, for the king,
this would be the last of his many labours
and triumphs in the world.
                    Then the wound
dealt by the ground-burner earlier began
to scald and swell; Beowulf discovered
deadly poison suppurating inside him,
surges of nausea, and so, in his wisdom
the prince realized his state and proceeded
towards a seat on the rampart. He steadied his gaze
on those gigantic stones, saw how the earthwork
was braced with arches built over columns.
And now that thane unequalled for goodness
with his own hands washed his lord's wounds,
swabbed the weary prince with water,
bathed him clean, unbuckled his helmet.

Beowulf senses
that he is near
death.

Beowulf spoke: in spite of his wounds,
mortal wounds, he still spoke
for he well knew his days in the world
had been lived out to the end: his allotted time
was drawing to a close, death was very near.

He thinks back on
his life.

'Now is the time when I would have wanted
to bestow this armour on my own son,
had it been my fortune to have fathered an heir
and live on in his flesh. For fifty years
I ruled this nation. No king
of any neighbouring clan would dare
face me with troops, none had the power
to intimidate me. I stood my ground
and took what came, cared for things in my keeping,
never fomented quarrels, never
swore to a lie. All this consoles me,
doomed as I am and sickening for death;
because of my right ways, the Ruler of mankind
need never blame me when the breath leaves my body

He bids Wiglaf to
inspect the hoard
and return with a
portion of the
treasure.

for murder of kinsmen. Go now quickly,
dearest Wiglaf, under the grey stone
where the dragon is laid out, lost to his treasure;
hurry to feast your eyes on the hoard.
Away you go: I want to examine
that ancient gold, gaze my fill
on those garnered jewels; my going will be easier
for having seen the treasure, a less troubled letting-go
of the life and lordship I have long maintained.'

Wiglaf enters the
dragon's barrow.

And so, I have heard, the son of Weohstan
quickly obeyed the command of his languishing
war-weary lord; he went in his chain-mail
under the rock-piled roof of the barrow,
exulting in his triumph, and saw beyond the seat

[2724–56]

a treasure-trove of astonishing richness,
wall-hangings that were a wonder to behold,
glittering gold spread across the ground,
the old dawn-scorching serpent's den
packed with goblets and vessels from the past,
tarnished and corroding. Rusty helmets
all eaten away. Artfully wrought
armbands everywhere. How easily can treasure
buried in the ground, gold hidden
however skilfully, escape from any man!

And he saw too a standard, entirely of gold,
hanging high over the hoard,
a masterpiece of filigree; it glowed with light
so he could make out the ground at his feet
and inspect the valuables. Of the dragon there was no
remaining sign: the sword had despatched him.
Then, the story goes, a certain man
plundered the hoard in that immemorial howe,
filled his arms with flagons and plates,
anything he wanted; and took the standard also,
most brilliant of banners.
                              Already the blade
of the old king's sharp killing-sword
had done its worst: the one who had for long
minded the hoard, hovering over gold,
unleashing fire, surging forth
midnight after midnight, had been mown down.

Wiglaf went quickly, keen to get back,   He returns with
excited by the treasure. Anxiety weighed   treasure.
on his brave heart, he was hoping he would find
the leader of the Geats alive where he had left him
helpless, earlier, on the open ground.

So he came to the place, carrying the treasure,

and found his lord bleeding profusely,
his life at an end; again he began
to swab his body. The beginnings of an utterance
heaved up from the coffers of the king's heart.
The old lord gazed sadly at the gold.

Beowulf gives thanks and orders the construction of a barrow to commemorate him.

'To the everlasting Lord of all,
to the King of Glory, I give thanks
that I behold this treasure here in front of me,
that I have thus been allowed to leave my people
so well endowed on the day I die.
Now that I have bartered my last breath
to own this fortune, it is up to you
to look after their needs. I can hold out no longer.
Order my troop to construct a barrow
on a headland on the coast, after my pyre has cooled.
It will loom on the horizon at Hronesness
and be a reminder among my people –
so that in coming times crews under sail
will call it Beowulf's Barrow, as they steer
ships across the wide and shrouded waters.'

Beowulf's last words.

Then the king in his great-heartedness unclasped
the collar of gold from his neck and gave it
to the young thane, telling him to use
it and the war-shirt and the gilded helmet well.

'You are the last of us, the only one left
of the Waegmundings. Fate swept us away,
sent my whole brave high-born clan
to their final doom. Now I must follow them.'

That was the warrior's last word.
He had no more to confide. The furious heat
of the pyre would assail him. His soul fled from his breast
to its destined place among the steadfast ones.

[2789–820]

It was hard then on the young hero,
having to watch the one he held so dear
there on the ground, going through
his death agony. The dragon from under-earth,
his nightmarish destroyer, lay destroyed as well,
utterly without life. No longer would his snakefolds
ply themselves to guard gold in the hoard:
hard-edged blades, hammered out
and keenly filed, had finished him
so that the sky-roamer lay there rigid,
brought low beside the treasure lodge.

The dragon too has
been destroyed.

Never again would he glitter and glide
and show himself off in midnight air,
exulting in his riches: he fell to earth
through the battle-strength in Beowulf's arm.
There were few, indeed, as far as I have heard,
big and brave as they may have been,
few who would have held out if they had had to face
the outpourings of that poison-breather
or gone foraging on the ring-hall floor
and found the deep barrow-dweller
on guard and awake.
                    The treasure had been won,
bought and paid for by Beowulf's death.
Both had reached the end of the road
through the life they had been lent.

                              Before long
the battle-dodgers abandoned the wood,
the ones who had let down their lord earlier,
the tail-turners, ten of them together.
When he needed them most, they had made off.
Now they were ashamed and came behind shields,
in their battle-outfits, to where the old man lay.

The battle-dodgers
come back.

They watched Wiglaf, sitting worn out,
a comrade shoulder to shoulder with his lord,
trying in vain to bring him round with water.
Much as he wanted to, there was no way
he could preserve his lord's life on earth
or alter in the least the Almighty's will.
What God judged right would rule what happened
to every man, as it does to this day.

Wiglaf rebukes
them.
Then a stern rebuke was bound to come
from the young warrior to the ones who had been cowards.
Wiglaf, son of Weohstan, spoke
disdainfully and in disappointment:
'Anyone ready to admit the truth
will surely realize that the lord of men
who showered you with gifts and gave you the armour
you are standing in – when he would distribute
helmets and mail-shirts to men on the mead-benches,
a prince treating his thanes in hall
to the best he could find, far or near –
was throwing weapons uselessly away.
It would be a sad waste when the war broke out.
The king had little cause to brag
about his armed guard; yet God who ordains
who wins or loses allowed him to strike
with his own blade when bravery was needed.
There was little I could do to protect his life
in the heat of the fray, but I found new strength
welling up when I went to help him.
Then my sword connected and the deadly assaults
of our foe grew weaker, the fire coursed
less strongly from his head. But when the worst happened
too few rallied around the prince.

So it is goodbye now to all you know and love
on your home ground, the open-handedness,

the giving of war-swords. Every one of you
with freeholds of land, our whole nation,
will be dispossessed, once princes from beyond
get tidings of how you turned and fled
and disgraced yourselves. A warrior will sooner
die than live a life of shame.'

He predicts that
enemies will now
attack the Geats.

Then he ordered the outcome of the fight to be reported
to those camped on the ridge, that crowd of retainers
who had sat all morning, sad at heart,
shield-bearers wondering about
the man they loved: would this day be his last
or would he return? He told the truth
and did not balk, the rider who bore
news to the cliff-top. He addressed them all:
'Now the people's pride and love,
the lord of the Geats, is laid on his deathbed,
brought down by the dragon's attack.
Beside him lies the bane of his life,
dead from knife-wounds. There was no way
Beowulf could manage to get the better
of the monster with his sword. Wiglaf sits
at Beowulf's side, the son of Weohstan,
the living warrior watching by the dead,
keeping weary vigil, holding a wake
for the loved and the loathed.

A messenger tells
the people that
Beowulf is dead.

　　　　　　　　　　　　Now war is looming
over our nation, soon it will be known
to Franks and Frisians, far and wide,
that the king is gone. Hostility has been great
among the Franks since Hygelac sailed forth
at the head of a war-fleet into Friesland:
there the Hetware harried and attacked
and overwhelmed him with great odds.
The leader in his war-gear was brought low,
fell amongst followers; that lord did not favour

He foresees wars
with the Franks and
the Frisians.

his company with spoils. The Merovingian king
has been an enemy to us ever since.

The Swedes too
will strike to
avenge the
slaughter of
Ongentheow.
'Nor do I expect peace or pact-keeping
of any sort from the Swedes. Remember:
at Ravenswood, Ongentheow
slaughtered Haethcyn, Hrethel's son,
when the Geat people in their arrogance
first attacked the fierce Shylfings.
The return blow was quickly struck
by Ohthere's father. Old and terrible,
he felled the sea-king and saved his own
aged wife, the mother of Onela
and of Ohthere, bereft of her gold rings.

Ongentheow's last
engagement at
Ravenswood: he
cornered a
Geatish force.
Then he kept hard on the heels of the foe
and drove them, leaderless, lucky to get away,
in a desperate rout into Ravenswood.
His army surrounded the weary remnant
where they nursed their wounds; all through the night
he howled threats at those huddled survivors,
promised to axe their bodies open
when dawn broke, dangle them from gallows
to feed the birds. But at first light
when their spirits were lowest, relief arrived.

Hygelac relieved
the besieged Geats.
They heard the sound of Hygelac's horn,
his trumpet calling as he came to find them,
the hero in pursuit, at hand with troops.

'The bloody swathe that Swedes and Geats
cut through each other was everywhere.
No one could miss their murderous feuding.
Then the old man made his move,
pulled back, barred his people in:

Ongentheow
withdrew.
Ongentheow withdrew to higher ground.
Hygelac's pride and prowess as a fighter
were known to the earl; he had no confidence

that he could hold out against that horde of seamen,
defend wife and the ones he loved
from the shock of the attack. He retreated for shelter
behind the earthwall. Then Hygelac swooped
on the Swedes at bay, his banners swarmed
into their refuge, his Geat forces
drove forward to destroy the camp.
There in his grey hairs, Ongentheow
was cornered, ringed around with swords.
And it came to pass that the king's fate
was in Eofor's hands, and in his alone.
Wulf, son of Wonred, went for him in anger,
split him open so that blood came spurting
from under his hair. The old hero
still did not flinch, but parried fast,
hit back with a harder stroke:
the king turned and took him on.
Then Wonred's son, the brave Wulf,
could land no blow against the aged lord.
Ongentheow divided his helmet
so that he buckled and bowed his bloodied head
and dropped to the ground. But his doom held off.
Though he was cut deep, he recovered again.

'With his brother down, the undaunted Eofor,
Hygelac's thane, hefted his sword
and smashed murderously at the massive helmet
past the lifted shield. And the king collapsed,
the shepherd of people was sheared of life.

'Many then hurried to help Wulf,
bandaged and lifted him, now that they were left
masters of the blood-soaked battleground.
One warrior stripped the other,
looted Ongentheow's iron mail-coat,
his hard sword-hilt, his helmet too,

The Swedish king
fought for his life.
He survived a blow
from Wulf, hit
back, but was killed
by Wulf's brother,
Eofor.

and carried the graith to King Hygelac;

The victorious
Geats returned
home.

he accepted the prize, promised fairly
that reward would come, and kept his word.
For their bravery in action, when they arrived home
Eofor and Wulf were overloaded
by Hrethel's son, Hygelac the Geat,
with gifts of land and linked rings
that were worth a fortune. They had won glory,
so there was no gainsaying his generosity.
And he gave Eofor his only daughter
to bide at home with him, an honour and a bond.

The messenger
predicts that the
Swedes will soon
retaliate.

'So this bad blood between us and the Swedes,
this vicious feud, I am convinced,
is bound to revive; they will cross our borders
and attack in force when they find out
that Beowulf is dead. In days gone by
when our warriors fell and we were undefended
he kept our coffers and our kingdom safe.
He worked for the people, but as well as that
he behaved like a hero.

With Beowulf gone,
a tragic future
awaits.

                              We must hurry now
to take a last look at the king
and launch him, lord and lavisher of rings,
on the funeral road. His royal pyre
will melt no small amount of gold:
heaped there in a hoard, it was bought at heavy cost,
and that pile of rings he paid for at the end
with his own life will go up with the flame,
be furled in fire: treasure no follower
will wear in his memory, nor lovely woman
link and attach as a torque around her neck –
but often, repeatedly, in the path of exile
they shall walk bereft, bowed under woe,
now that their leader's laugh is silenced,
high spirits quenched. Many a spear

[2988–3021]

dawn-cold to the touch will be taken down
and waved on high; the swept harp
won't waken warriors, but the raven winging
darkly over the doomed will have news,
tidings for the eagle of how he hoked and ate,
how he and the wolf made short work of the dead.'

Such was the drift of the dire report
that gallant man delivered. He got little wrong
in what he told and predicted.
                              The whole troop

The Geats find the
two bodies.

rose in tears, then took their way
to the uncanny scene under Earnaness.
There, on the sand, where his soul had left him,
they found him at rest, their ring-giver
from days gone by. The great man
had breathed his last. Beowulf the king
had indeed met with a marvellous death.

But what they saw first was far stranger:
the serpent on the ground, gruesome and vile,
lying facing him. The fire-dragon
was scaresomely burnt, scorched all colours.
From head to tail, his entire length
was fifty feet. He had shimmered forth
on the night air once, then winged back
down to his den; but death owned him now,
he would never enter his earth-gallery again.
Beside him stood pitchers and piled-up dishes,
silent flagons, precious swords
eaten through with rust, ranged as they had been
while they waited their thousand winters under ground.
That huge cache, gold inherited
from an ancient race, was under a spell –
which meant no one was ever permitted
to enter the ring-hall unless God Himself,

mankind's keeper, True King of Triumphs,
allowed some person pleasing to Him –
and in His eyes worthy – to open the hoard.

What came about brought to nothing
the hopes of the one who had wrongly hidden
riches under the rock-face. First the dragon slew
that man among men, who in turn made fierce amends
and settled the feud. Famous for his deeds
a warrior may be, but it remains a mystery
where his life will end, when he may no longer
dwell in the mead-hall among his own.
So it was with Beowulf, when he faced the cruelty
and cunning of the mound-guard. He himself was ignorant
of how his departure from the world would happen.
The high-born chiefs who had buried the treasure
declared it until doomsday so accursed
that those who robbed it would be guilty of wrong
and grimly punished for their transgression,
hasped in hell-bonds in heathen shrines.
Yet Beowulf's gaze at the gold treasure
when he first saw it had not been selfish.

Wiglaf ponders
Beowulf's fate.

Wiglaf, son of Weohstan, spoke:
'Often when one man follows his own will
many are hurt. This happened to us.
Nothing we advised could ever convince
the prince we loved, our land's guardian,
not to vex the custodian of the gold,
let him lie where he was long accustomed,
lurk there under earth until the end of the world.
He held to his high destiny. The hoard is laid bare,
but at a grave cost; it was too cruel a fate
that forced the king to that encounter.
I have been inside and seen everything
amassed in the vault. I managed to enter

[3055–88]

although no great welcome awaited me
under the earthwall. I quickly gathered up
a huge pile of the priceless treasures
handpicked from the hoard and carried them here
where the king could see them. He was still himself,
alive, aware, and in spite of his weakness
he had many requests. He wanted me to greet you He reports
Beowulf's last
wishes.
and order the building of a barrow that would crown
the site of his pyre, serve as his memorial,
in a commanding position, since of all men
to have lived and thrived and lorded it on earth
his worth and due as a warrior were the greatest.
Now let us again go swiftly
and feast our eyes on that amazing fortune
heaped under the wall. I will show the way
and bring you close to those coffers packed with rings
and bars of gold. Let a bier be made
and got ready quickly when we come out
and then let us bring the body of our lord,
the man we loved, to where he will lodge
for a long time in the care of the Almighty.'

Then Weohstan's son, stalwart to the end, Wiglaf gives orders
for the building of a
funeral pyre.
had orders given to owners of dwellings,
many people of importance in the land,
to fetch wood from far and wide
for the good man's pyre.
              'Now shall flame consume
our leader in battle, the blaze darken
round him who stood his ground in the steel-hail,
when the arrow-storm shot from bowstrings
pelted the shield-wall. The shaft hit home.
Feather-fledged, it finned the barb in flight.'

Next the wise son of Weohstan He goes with seven
thanes to remove
called from among the king's thanes

a group of seven: he selected the best
and entered with them, the eighth of their number,
under the God-cursed roof; one raised
a lighted torch and led the way.
No lots were cast for who should loot the hoard
since it was obvious to them that every bit of it
lay unprotected within the vault,
there for the taking. It was no trouble
to hurry to work and haul out
the priceless store. They pitched the dragon
over the cliff-top, let tide's flow
and backwash take the treasure-minder.
Then coiled gold was loaded on a cart
in great abundance, and the grey-haired leader,
the prince on his bier, was borne to Hronesness.

Beowulf's funeral. The Geat people built a pyre for Beowulf,
stacked and decked it until it stood foursquare,
hung with helmets, heavy war-shields
and shining armour, just as he had ordered.
Then his warriors laid him in the middle of it,
mourning a lord far-famed and beloved.
On a height they kindled the hugest of all
funeral fires; fumes of woodsmoke
billowed darkly up, the blaze roared
and drowned out their weeping, wind died down
and flames wrought havoc in the hot bone-house,
burning it to the core. They were disconsolate
and wailed aloud for their lord's decease.

A Geat woman's
dread. A Geat woman too sang out in grief;
with hair bound up, she unburdened herself
of her worst fears, a wild litany
of nightmare and lament: her nation invaded,
enemies on the rampage, bodies in piles,
slavery and abasement. Heaven swallowed the smoke.

Then the Geat people began to construct Beowulf's barrow.
a mound on a headland, high and imposing,
a marker that sailors could see from afar,
and in ten days they had done the work.
It was their hero's memorial; what remained from the fire
they housed inside it, behind a wall
as worthy of him as their workmanship could make it.
And they buried torques in the barrow, and jewels
and a trove of such things as trespassing men
had once dared to drag from the hoard.
They let the ground keep that ancestral treasure,
gold under gravel, gone to earth,
as useless to men now as it ever was.
Then twelve warriors rode around the tomb,
chieftains' sons, champions in battle,
all of them distraught, chanting in dirges, His people lament.
mourning his loss as a man and a king.
They extolled his heroic nature and exploits
and gave thanks for his greatness; which was the proper thing
for a man should praise a prince whom he holds dear
and cherish his memory when that moment comes
when he has to be convoyed from his bodily home.
So the Geat people, his hearth-companions,
sorrowed for the lord who had been laid low.
They said that of all the kings upon the earth
he was the man most gracious and fair-minded,
kindest to his people and keenest to win fame.

FAMILY TREES

Family trees of the Danish, Swedish and Geatish dynasties. Names given here are the ones used in this translation.

THE DANES OR THE SHIELDINGS

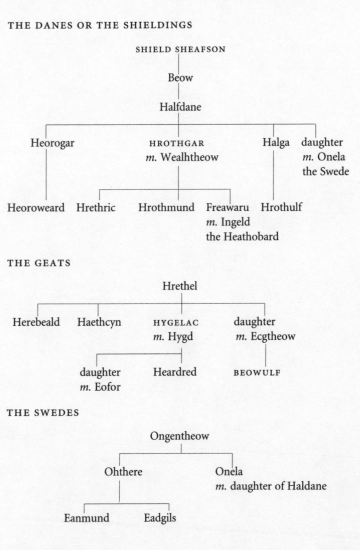

SHIELD SHEAFSON
|
Beow
|
Halfdane

Heorogar — HROTHGAR *m.* Wealhtheow — Halga — daughter *m.* Onela the Swede

Heoroweard — Hrethric — Hrothmund — Freawaru *m.* Ingeld the Heathobard — Hrothulf

THE GEATS

Hrethel

Herebeald — Haethcyn — HYGELAC *m.* Hygd — daughter *m.* Ecgtheow

daughter *m.* Eofor — Heardred — BEOWULF

THE SWEDES

Ongentheow

Ohthere — Onela *m.* daughter of Haldane

Eanmund — Eadgils

A NOTE ON NAMES

by Professor Alfred David, reprinted here by kind permission of W. W. Norton & Co.

Old English, like Modern German, contained many compound words, most of which have been lost in Modern English. Most of the names in *Beowulf* are compounds. Hrothgar is a combination of words meaning 'glory' and 'spear'; the name of his older brother, Heorogar, comes from 'army' and 'spear'; Hrothgar's sons Hrethric and Hrothmund contain the first elements of their father's name combined, respectively, with *ric* (kingdom, empire, Modern German *Reich*) and *mund* (hand, protection). As in the case of the Danish dynasty, family names often alliterate. Masculine names of the warrior class have military associations. The importance of family and the demands of alliteration frequently lead to the designation of characters by formulas identifying them in terms of relationships. Thus Beowulf is referred to as 'son of Ecgtheow' or 'kinsman of Hygelac' (his uncle and lord).

The Old English spellings of names are mostly preserved in the translation. A few rules of pronunciation are worth keeping in mind. Initial *H* before *r* was sounded, and so Hrothgar's name alliterates with that of his brother Heorogar. The combination *sc* has the value of *sh* in Scylding and Scylfing. The combination *cg* has the value of *dg* in words like 'edge'. The first element in the name of Beowulf's father 'Ecgtheow' is the same word as 'edge', and, by the figure of speech called synechdoche (a part of something stands for the whole), *ecg* stands for *sword* and Ecgtheow means 'sword-servant'.

ACKNOWLEDGEMENTS

The proposal that I should translate *Beowulf* came in the early 1980s from the editors of *The Norton Anthology of English Literature*, so my first thanks go to M. H. Abrams and Jon Stallworthy who encouraged the late John Benedict to commission some preliminary passages. Then, when I got going in earnest four years ago, Norton appointed Professor Alfred David to keep a learned eye on what I was making of the original; without his annotations on the first draft and his many queries and suggested alternatives as the manuscript advanced towards completion, this translation would have been a weaker and a wobblier thing. Al's responses were informed by scholarship and by a lifetime's experience of teaching the poem, so they were invaluable. Nevertheless, I was often reluctant to follow his advice and persisted many times in what we both knew were erroneous ways, so he is not responsible for any failures here in the construing of the original or for the different directions in which it is occasionally skewed.

I am also grateful to W. W. Norton & Co. for allowing the translation to be published by Faber and Faber in London and by Farrar, Straus & Giroux in New York. The Anglo-Saxon on p. 2 is reprinted by kind permission from *Beowulf: A Student Edition*, edited by George Jack (Clarendon Press, 1994).

At Faber, I benefited greatly from Christopher Reid's editorial pencil on the first draft and Paul Keegan's on the second. I also had important encouragement and instruction in the latter stages of the work from colleagues at Harvard, who now include by happy coincidence the present Associate General Editor of *The Norton Anthology*, Professor Stephen Greenblatt. I remember with special pleasure a medievalists' seminar where I finally recanted on the use of the word 'gilly' in the presence of Professors Larry Benson, Dan Donoghue, Joseph Harris and Derek Pearsall. Professor John R. Niles happened to attend that seminar and I was lucky to enjoy another, too brief discussion with him in Berkeley, worrying about word-choices and wondering about the prejudice in favour of Anglo-Saxon over Latinate diction in translations of the poem.

Helen Vendler's reading helped, as ever, in many points of detail, and I received other particular and important comments from Professor Mary Clayton, Marijane Osborn and Peter Sacks.

Extracts from the first hundred lines of the translation appeared in *The Haw Lantern* (1987) and in *Causley at 70* (1987). Excerpts from the more recent work were published in *Agni, The Sunday Times, The Threepenny Review, The Times Literary Supplement*; also in *A Parcel of Poems: for Ted Hughes on his Sixty-Fifth Birthday* and *The Literary Man, Essays Presented to Donald W. Hannah*. Lines 88–98 were printed in January 1999 by Bow & Arrow Press as a tribute to Professor William Alfred, himself a translator of the poem and, while he lived, one of the great teachers of it. Bits of the Introduction first appeared in *The Sunday Times* and in an article entitled 'Further Language' (*Studies in Literary Imagination*, Volume xxx, No. 2). The epigraph to the Introduction is from my poem 'The Settle Bed' (*Seeing Things*, 1991). The broken lines on p. 71 indicate lacunae in the original text.

S. H.